EDUCATION FOR HUMAN DEVELOPMENT

EDUCATION FOR HUMAN DEVELOPMENT

Understanding Montessori

MARIO M. MONTESSORI, JR.

Edited by Paula Polk Lillard

Schocken Books • New York

First published by SCHOCKEN BOOKS 1976

Copyright © 1976 by Schocken Books Inc.

Library of Congress Cataloging in Publication Data

Montessori, Mario M
    Education for human development.

    Includes index.
    1. Montessori method of education. I. Title.

LB775.M8M37   372.1′3   75-37042

Manufactured in the United States of America

To My Children
Mario, Carolina, Ada, Nicolina, *and* Rolando

CONTENTS

AN APPRECIATION
OF MONTESSORI
Buckminster Fuller

All children are born geniuses. 9999 out of every 10,000 are swiftly, inadvertently, degeniused by grown-ups. This happens because human beings are born naked, helpless, and—though superbly equipped cerebrally—utterly lacking in experience, therefore utterly ignorant. Their delicate sensing equipment is, as yet, untried. Born with built-in hunger, thirst, curiosity, the procreative urge, they can only learn what humanity has learned by trial and error—by billions upon billions of errors. Yet humanity is also endowed with self-deceiving pride. All those witnessing the errors of others proclaim that they (the witnesses) could have prevented those errors had they only been consulted. "People should not make mistakes" they mistakenly say. Motivated entirely by love, but also by fear for the futures of the children they love, parents, in their ignorance, act as though they know all the answers and curtail the spontaneous exploratory acts of their children, lest the children make "mistakes." But genius does its own thinking; it has confidence in its own exploratory findings, in its own intuitions, in the knowledge gained from its own mistakes. Nature has her own gestation rates for evolutionary development. The actions of parents represent the checks and balances of nature's gestation control. Humanity can evolve healthily only at a given rate. Maria Montessori was fortunately permitted to maintain, sustain, and cultivate her innate genius. Her genius invoked her awareness of the genius inherent in all children. Her intuition and initiative inspired her to discover ways of safeguarding this genius while allaying the ignorant fears of parents. But the way was not always easy. Hers was the difficult frontiering task of genius.

BUCKMINSTER FULLER

Sunset, Maine
August 19, 1975

INTRODUCTION
Paula Polk Lillard

Maria Montessori began her pioneering work on behalf of children at the turn of the century. The centennial of her birth was celebrated not long ago. However, during the intervening years, there have been fewer commentaries adding new insights to her work than one would expect.[1] The following chapters help to fill this void in the Montessori literature. They are based on lectures originally presented, for the most part, at Montessori meetings in various countries during the 1960s and 1970s by Dr. Mario M. Montessori, Jr., a practicing psychoanalyst in Amsterdam, vice president of the International Psychoanalytic Association, and a grandson of Maria Montessori. These lectures, given in English, were prepared in response to requests from Montessori teachers and parents for information on various topics. They represent an endeavor on the author's part to highlight the originality of some of Montessori's viewpoints and show their importance for education today.

One fact is clear from the essays in this book: Montessori was calling for a revolution in society's approach to human development and education. Because of her revolutionary ideas, Montessori's philosophy and methods historically have not been easily understood or accepted, by either her critics or her admirers. One area in which her revolutionary approach is apparent is in her attitude to the child himself.

Montessori had a deep reverence for creation. This reverence and her knowledge of the physical sciences combined in a focus on children and their role in the creation of adult human beings. Phillipe Aries points out in *Centuries of Childhood* [2] that the recognition of the child as a unique entity is relatively recent in Western culture. Historically, very young children were regarded as primitive beings to be physically cared for, but whose importance, except in the continuum of human life, was given little thought. As early as the age of seven or eight they were regarded as miniature adults, expected to reason, to accept responsibility, and often, to plan for their own survival.

Gradually, with the advent of the Industrial Revolution, a concern for the state of childhood began. Children played a more realistic role in the arts—in the novels of Charles Dickens and the paintings of the Impressionists. Society's new awareness of children may have been partly a result of the development of family life as we know it today, with parents, particularly mothers, able to spend more time in the home.[3] For the most part, however, this new awareness grew out of the psychological and cultural framework of nineteenth-century Europe and America. The traditional emphasis of the Christian Church on man's evil nature and the necessity for the salvation of children through baptism had led to an approach to children that was often one of rigid control and manipulation. However, at least one philosopher, Rousseau, had taken an opposite view—that children were innately good and needed only to be freed from the contamination of civilization for their true nature to be exposed. This theory often contributed to a sentimental and idealistic view of the child. To add to the confusion, Freud's work with adults had revealed the sexuality of the very young child. Adults, made aware of their own repressed emotions, became less sure of how children should be treated.

The varied approaches to children current in the nineteenth century had one aspect in common. They were based, for the most part, on the experience of adults with other adults. They were not derived from direct observation of the behavior and development of children. Montessori, however, reasoned that the way to a deeper understanding of men and women was through observation of children.

The child should not be regarded as a feeble and helpless creature whose only need is to be protected and helped, but as a spiritual embryo, possessed of an active psychic life from the day that he is born and guided by subtle instincts enabling him to actively build up the human personality. And since it is the child who becomes the adult man, we must consider him as the true builder of mankind and recognize him as our father. The great secret of our origin lies hidden within him, and the laws that will lead man to his rightful state of being can be manifested only within him. In this sense the child is our teacher.[4]

Dr. Montessori's medical background led her logically to this conclusion. She noted that biologists had not really understood organisms from studying them in their fully developed state. Only after the invention of the microscope and the observation of cell division was a breakthrough in embryology, and hence in biology, made. By the same token, it was not until physical scientists could peer into the atomic "window," the spectrum, that a breakthrough in the understanding of matter came.

Although trained in the scientific approach, Montessori did not pursue her study of the child in the necessarily restricted environment of the laboratory. This fact has caused misunderstanding, even mistrust, of Montessori's work. It may be well, therefore, to let her speak for herself in explaining what thoughts went through her mind when she worked with children.

When I am in the midst of children I do not think of myself as a scientist, a theoretician. When I am with children I am a nobody, and the greatest privilege I have when I approach them is being able to forget that I even exist, for this has enabled me to see things that one would miss if one were somebody—little things, simple but very precious truths. It is not always imperative to see big things, but it is of paramount importance to see the beginnings of things. At their origins there are little glimmers that can be recognized as soon as something new is developing. . . . The child is a spiritual embryo that develops spontaneously, and if we follow him from the beginning, he can reveal many things to us.[5]

This thought introduces a second revolutionary approach of Montessori; it is the humanity of children at which we must look in order to discover the secret of their life. What is specifically human about children, the spontaneous nature of these developing spiritual embryos, cannot be uncovered in the strict scientific atmosphere of the laboratory.

There are, of course, scientists who have studied the likenesses between men and animals in the laboratory: Darwin and Wallace, and more recently, Lorenz and Skinner. Although what they tell us can be useful, we should not exaggerate the help behavioral psychologists can give us. It is the uniqueness of man that we must penetrate if we are to solve the problems of our existence. As Montessori points out,

> Man's soul is an enigma. It has remained an unknown that inhabits an unknown domain. Not even psychology has been able to enlighten us, to shed light on the mystery.[6]

Since the 1960s there has been a shift away from the emphasis on laboratory techniques and animal research in the study of man. The discovery by biologists that we are not what we thought we were, even physically,[7] and by physicists that all matter evolves, has ended the age-old dream that the universe and our observations of it can be reduced to precise mathematical formulas. As Bronowski notes in *The Ascent of Man*,

> we had hoped that human errors would disappear and that we would ourselves have God's view. But it turns out that the errors cannot be taken out of the observations. And that is true of stars, or atoms, or just looking at somebody's picture, or hearing the report of somebody's speech.[8]

This new humility toward the results of laboratory research may result in a more receptive attitude toward Montessori's approach to the study of the child. For, though she was a careful experimenter and keen observer, she had no expectations of reducing her contribution to irrefutable scientific theories through laboratory procedures. Her concentration on the uniqueness of man and his spontaneous development precluded any such dream. Rather than arguing the scientific merits of her work, it may be more useful to consider it as belonging to the realm of natural philosophy: an area of study somewhat neglected in recent years perhaps, but one that is once again beginning to receive attention—even from scientists.[9]

Dr. Mario Jr. also discusses two further revolutionary concepts of Maria Montessori in his lectures: her view of education as a necessity in the formation of the human personality and the relationship of man to the cosmos. Her development of "cosmic education" in response to her convictions concerning the latter is particularly important for our world today.

Education for Human Development succeeds in conveying the depth of Maria Montessori's contribution to human knowledge as no book before it has done. Montessori made revolutionary discoveries regarding human development that have implications far beyond a simple shift to new educational approaches or techniques. The author's unique background, combining as it does psychoanalytic experience and an intimate knowledge of Montessori, has made possible an articulate discussion of these discoveries and their relation to the problems and opportunities of the modern world. His discussion of modern psychology and psychoanalytic concepts as they relate to Montessori, and of the role of work and play in the development of human personality, are particularly outstanding.

Because the original audience for Mario Jr.'s lectures were Montessori parents and teachers, they presuppose some working knowledge of classroom procedures. For those who may not have such knowledge, an appendix containing impressions from a morning visit to two classes in a Montessori school has been included. Hopefully, it will convey to the reader at least the flavor of Montessori classroom life.

PAULA POLK LILLARD

NOTES

1. One notable exception is J. McVicker Hunt's excellent, but necessarily brief, introduction to the American edition of *The Montessori Method*, published by Schocken Books in 1964. Also see M. M. Montessori, *Montessori Method—Science or Belief?* (Amsterdam: A. M. I. Communications, 1968), p. 8.

2. Phillipe Ariés, *Centuries of Childhood* (New York: Knopf, 1962).

3. Elizabeth Janeway, *Man's World, Women's Place* (New York: Arno, 1973).

4. Maria Montessori, *Education and Peace* (Chicago: Regnery, 1972), p. 41.

5. Ibid., p. 101.

6. Ibid., p. 103.

7. See Thomas Lewis, *The Lives of a Cell* (New York: Viking, 1974).

8. J. Bronowski, *The Ascent of Man* (Boston: Little Brown, 1973), pp. 13, 15, 364.

9. Montessori, *Education and Peace*, p. 90.

EDUCATION FOR HUMAN DEVELOPMENT

1/ THE CONTRIBUTION OF MARIA MONTESSORI

Maria Montessori was originally no pedagogue, but a physician with a deep interest in the human person, both as a social being and as a participant in the fundamental ontological order. In the course of her career as the first woman physician in Italy, and later as Professor of Anthropology and Hygienics at the University of Rome, she actively participated in the emancipation of women. She enjoyed an international reputation for a decade before the onset of the educational experiment with which she eventually came to be identified by society. She gained world fame as a pedagogue, yet this role, and its instantaneous effect on public opinion, actually took her as much by surprise as did the discoveries on which it was based. It was insight into the significance of these discoveries for a better understanding of the human being that motivated her subsequent behavior. It compelled her, on the one hand, to concentrate on this particular investigation to the exclusion of everything else, and on the other, to communicate her findings to her fellow men and to fight whatever prevented their acceptance.

This attitude generated from the start a cultural movement of growing impact, one that is still going on. It was not Montessori's intention to start such a movement; it was merely a byproduct of her activities. Her concern was to bring to light her newly acquired knowledge of human development. She dedicated herself whole-heartedly to this task, advocating the cause of the child (i.e., of man in becoming) throughout her long life.

1

Because her experiences indicated that education played a more essential role in this process of becoming than was generally assumed, Montessori focused her attention on this particular realm of human activity. Hence her reputation as a pedagogue. However, her approach was so radically different from what is generally encountered in the pedagogical world that it is questionable whether the label really fits her. I believe this to be one source of the many controversies that have arisen in connection with her work. It is, in any case, certain that she herself never fully identified with the role of pedagogue nor, for that matter, with many other images that have been projected on her. She followed her own course, guided by what had impressed her as a basic truth, so far ignored, that should be brought to the attention of those concerned with the human situation. So intent was she on her purpose that she took little notice of either the ensuing praise or criticism of her activities. Her goal was to enable others to see the basic truth she had discovered, so that they could be guided by it in their own way regardless of what they thought of her or her method.

In regard to her method, she was indeed strict in requesting those who wished to apply it in her name to follow her directions. They would otherwise confuse the issue with regard to her own experiment. However, her contribution to human knowledge had a broader scope, and has had a wider influence, than what is generally known as Montessori education. Even if we consider only the applications of the latter, it is clear that her position as a pedagogue is unique compared with that of other educators. A brief survey of the Montessori movement shows growth and development in three different directions. Its horizontal growth is evident from the Montessori schools and training institutes found throughout the world. Montessori's books have been translated into twenty-two languages, and interest in her work continues to spread. But these achievements are only geographical. More interesting is the ramification of applications of her method beyond the realm of regular school education. The Montessori approach is followed in homes, in child care centers, in work with the hospitalized, the maladjusted, the crippled and otherwise handicapped children, in teaching the socially deprived and the mentally retarded, in educating the blind, and in combating analphabetism in adults. Its restriction in some areas is also interesting. Montessori education has been forbidden in totalitarian countries. Montessori schools were closed in Russia after the revolution, and in Germany and Italy at the height of imperialism. Few, if any, educational systems have received this kind of attention from politicians.

The vertical growth of the Montessori movement is clear from the extension of its application from the upbringing of infants to the education of children up to university age, and the only reason the Montessori approach is not in use in universities is because no opportunity to put it into practice at that level has occurred. The Montessori method is applicable in all social strata, among the population of the ghettos and slums, among the middle class, among the very rich, and in public as well as in private institutions.

A third direction in which growth has occurred is through time. The Montessori movement has, since its inception, retained its spontaneous character, its freshness, and its stamina, notwithstanding much direct opposition. In many areas where it had flourished, wars or changes in the cultural climate paralyzed its course, or even eliminated it altogether, for long periods. Sooner or later, however, it reappeared with new impetus and strength. A typical example is its revival in the United States. After having been abandoned and largely forgotten for many years, the Montessori approach was revived in the late 1950s. There are over three thousand Montessori schools in the United States today, and the number increases rapidly each year. Montessori education is equally in demand in the developing countries of the world. It appears, then, to have a promising future; its major concern at the moment is not one of gaining acceptance, but of training sufficient numbers of persons to cope adequately with its own growth.

What I have hoped to point out here is the exceptional position of Montessori education in the pedagogical world. I do not believe that there is any other method of education that can serve the objectives of all the different situations I have mentioned. Clearly, then, there must be something unusual about this one. It is certainly not that it can offer empirical evidence of success in all those fields in which it has been adopted. Montessori originally worked only with small children. Later, she also worked with those in elementary schools, but her pedagogical experience stopped there. Nor is it because her views are so clearly formulated or easily understood that her approach has such wide appeal. She was not a theoretician. She did not construct a differentiated theoretical framework that paved the way for later applications of her work. On the contrary, in her struggle to give expression to phenomena that did not fit any existing theories, she often borrowed terms from them, dissociating them from their frame of reference and using them in her own context. This has been the source of many misinterpretations of her ideas by her critics. From the start, the Montessori movement has been accompanied by vivid discussions of her method ending in a variety of divergent views, ranging from strong opposition to fervent approval. An anthology of the most relevant of these contrasting opinions has recently been published in Germany.[1] What impresses one most in it is the renewed actuality of the method throughout the years.

What is it in Maria Montessori's work that can explain all these phenomena? If we turn to her for enlightenment, we find that her own conclusion was both simple and puzzling. She maintained that she had "discovered" the child. If, reflecting upon forty years' experience, Montessori condensed the essence of her contribution into this one phrase, then it is important to try to understand what she meant by it.

One of the striking qualities in Maria Montessori's personality was her deep respect for creation. She never ceased to marvel at its manifestations. In her philosophical outlook, man's cosmic task is to continue, collectively, the work of creation on earth, to discover with his intelligence the endless latent possibilities of the world's creations and make them manifest in new forms. It is in this way that man creates his cultural environment. This conception of man encompasses his potential greatness as a creator, as well as his smallness and limitations in relation to God and His creation. This deep-rooted conviction about human destiny, based on her faith in God and man, gave Dr. Montessori the moral strength to pursue her objectives in life. It was also the basis of the humility and respect with which she approached the world and her fellow men throughout her life.

It was in this spirit that she undertook further scientific study of children. They were to her fellow human beings who should be considered such. This attitude freed her of the common prejudices adults hold toward children and eventually enabled her to discover the extremely important function of the child in the formation of the human personality. This discovery was not made by philosophical methods. It was the direct result of careful, patient, and systematic observations of the spontaneous behavior of children in a prepared environment adapted to their needs—of a scientific experiment based on previous experiences and performed with the detached involvement typical of a scientifically groomed mind. Montessori's philosophical outlook, however, was responsible for her ability to see beyond the superficial manifestations of the children's behavior she observed. She distilled from them basic phenomena relevant to human development and integrated them into a comprehensive and coherent vision of man that took into account the full complexity of his existence on earth.

It was this anthropological orientation in its widest sense that determined Montessori's revolutionary conception of education as an aid to life, and it is to my mind the most valuable aspect of the spiritual inheritance she has left us.

Professor N. Perquin of the University of Nijmegen, in highlighting Montessori's contribution as the starting point of a new vision of education, remarks in this connection, "Without knowing it, she made possible an encounter between pedagogy, modern psychology, and sociology, even theology and philosophy." [2] Montessori's aim, from the start, had been to contribute to a comprehensive science of man. This science could not, according to her, be based on any single discipline, but should result from the concerted endeavors of different scientists studying human beings from whatever angles modern science permitted and the integration of their findings into a sufficiently broad and differentiated conceptual matrix. This integration should not be done in an eclectic manner, which would only confuse the issues. Rather, it should be based on a tentative blueprint encompassing the different fundamental aspects of the human situation. This global model should be related to findings from the different branches of science, and the modifications indicated by an investigation of their interrelationships should be made.

Although this pluralistic approach is by no means currently

accepted, tendencies toward a more articulate investigation acknowledging important differences in human behavior, and aiming at an integration of the relevant findings, are slowly winning ground in the human sciences.[3] Montessori herself contributed a blueprint for this investigation by the various sciences. One of its major aspects is the adaptive and constructive role of the child in human life. In one of her writings Montessori states that

> the great power of man is that he adapts to every part of the environment and that he modifies it. For this reason every man that is born must prepare his personality anew. There is no hereditary adaptation in individuals; each must develop something which corresponds to it. At birth a child does not have the behavior characteristics of the group into which he is born; he has to create and prepare them. He has to learn their language and the customs and the use of their implements, etc. In other words, while developing himself he unconsciously develops his own adaptation to his environment. To understand the child's tendencies with the purpose of educating him, we must see man in correlation with his environment and how his adaptation to it is created.[4]

This implies that human development is the result of an unconscious creative activity of the individual, and that this process is only possible in association with others. It is only in the community that man's potentialities can be realized. This is the work of the child, guided from within by special sensitivities inherent in the various stages of development.

Children need more than adults' love and protection to perform this double task of adaptation and construction. They need their active help. This implies that education is a fundamental aspect of the formation of man, a concept that will be dealt with at greater length in later chapters. It is sufficient here to mention that Montessori's conception of the nature of human experience envisaged the complexity of human beings and the numerous factors determining their behavior and further existence in real life, without ever losing sight of the unity of their personalities. Of course, she was not able to study all aspects of human development herself. Several of her ideas were inferred from her own experiences, others were conclusions based on her work, or conjectures based on

intuition, or mere glimmers of possible avenues of further investigation. It is for this reason that the term blueprint has been used with
regard to her theoretical formulations.

I consider it significant that Montessori's model of development
corresponds in the main with that arrived at by psychoanalysts. In
my experience, psychoanalysis is the only branch of empirical
science that has accepted the challenge of studying man with this
type of composite frame of reference. Neither Montessori nor
psychoanalysis tries to simplify or reduce the complexity of the
picture of man to fit a special theory. Instead, both acknowledge
the diversity of factors determining human development and
behavior. They endeavor to cope with them in concordance with
the findings obtained by observations of spontaneous behavior in a
specially prepared setting. The situation in both cases is so
structured that it activates certain aspects of behavior that would
not otherwise manifest themselves with the same clarity and
continuity. This makes it possible to study phenomena not noticed
before.

The situation is a complicated one in the sense that the same
person must function as an observer and as a participant in the
relationship that ensues. Another set of behavioral factors is
brought into play by the dynamics of the situation: in the case of
the classroom, those pertaining to the teacher. In addition, the
classroom situation involves a whole group of others as well. These
are necessary complications, however, for human behavior can only
be studied in the setting of human relations if it is to be considered
from the viewpoint of spontaneous development. We cannot avoid
this circumstance.

In both the psychoanalytic and the Montessori approach, the
relation of observer-participant and participant should be one of
alliance based on mutual respect and confidence. The observer-
participant should be carefully trained. He should be interested in
the phenomena he is observing and understand them. He should
allow situations to develop freely, abstaining from intervention
when it is not necessary and acting appropriately when it is. His
actions should be determined by the situation and its objectives,
never by his own impulses or wishes, which might interfere with the
process at hand. His aim should be to remove obstacles that inhibit

the natural course of events, to promote insights that further it, and to help work these through. His attitude should be one of empathy, cooperation, and patience.

Of course, the objectives of psychoanalysis and Montessori education are quite different, as is the material that is studied. Their findings, however, tend to confirm and to complement each other. It is especially significant that the models to which they lead have a similar structure. Montessori herself explicitly identified her method with psychoanalysis. Regarding modern pedagogy, which had previously been limited to the study of external phenomena, she remarked, "To borrow medical terminology, we might say that it was an attempt to cure the symptoms without seeking the essential but obscure cause." She then proceeded to illustrate the limitations of symptomatic therapy, contrasting it with psychoanalysis, which deals with the causes of behavior.[5] This similarity between Montessori education and psychoanalysis may, incidentally, explain the striking parallel in the vicissitudes each has encountered.

Montessori's view of the specificity of mankind as a species differs from that of the sciences, even psychology. To my knowledge, it is only that train of psychological thought based on philosophical anthropology, the influence of which is mainly confined to German-speaking countries, which departs explicitly from this assumption. Empirical psychology in general does not. Montessori's position in relation to it requires, therefore, some further consideration. Her medical studies gave a sound biological basis to her later conceptions of man's development and behavior, but they in no way shook her firm conviction of his specificity in relation to other living beings. One finds it postulated even in her doctor's thesis as the frame of reference for an otherwise purely clinical psychiatric treatise.[6] In her very last book she still held this position, stating that

What causes us to distinguish between species is always their differences, never their likeness. What constitutes another species is always something new. . . . The human species has a double embryonic life. . . . It is built to a new design, and has a fresh destiny in relation to the other creatures. . . . This is the point at which we must pause, and make a fresh start in all our studies of child development and of man's psychological side.[7]

Modern psychology has not yet made this start, although some tentative recent developments seem to indicate that it may yet do so. In the main, however, psychology is still strongly influenced by American behaviorism, which explicitly ignores the existence of a fundamental difference between man and other living beings. Behaviorism's impact on modern learning theory is particularly strong. But whatever merits this approach may have in highlighting certain features of human behavior that are common to other animals, and which can therefore, in principle, be studied through experiments with the latter, it is too limited in scope and too one-sided to further our understanding of the human being as such. It perforce excludes from investigation all aspects of his personality that cannot be encompassed within its artificially restricted frame of reference. If its findings are not integrated into a more comprehensive scientific conception of man, modern psychology and modern learning theory will have no contribution to offer in the solution of the ever-increasing social problems with which humanity is confronted in our technological era. These will always bring us back to the study of the individual personality in its own right. If one considers man as an animal and explicitly ignores those fundamental differences that distinguish the one from the other, one will convincingly demonstrate that man is, for all practical purposes, just a naked ape, as Desmond Morris has so entertainingly demonstrated.[8] However, the resulting conception of man will be restricted and distorted, and therefore unscientific.

In seeking to understand the uniqueness of mankind as a species, a distinction should be made between growth and development. These two concepts are often confused or misused in modern psychology, leading to ambiguous or arbitrary conclusions in some studies. For example, consider the findings of Coghill,[9] who has made such a marvelous analysis of his concise anatomical studies in relation to behavior, and Bruner,[10] who has carefully studied relevant patterns in the unfolding of intelligence as a basis for a theory of instruction. Both use these two concepts alternatively, writing of the growth when, in fact, they should refer to the process involved as development. I do not believe that this is because they would not understand, or could not accept, the difference between the two. Nor do I believe that their choice of one term rather than the other is random, although they may not be conscious of their motivations. Whatever the case may be, the terms they use influence their conclusions, even if in different degrees, and affect their contribution to a better understanding of human behavior.

What *is* the difference between growth and development? Growth implies only an enlargement or self-multiplication of an existing form. Carrel describes, for example, the cellular colonies proceeding from a particle of the heart of the embryo of a chicken, which continued to multiply for a period of twenty-three years in a controlled environment. The modifications in the original are only quantitative, not qualitative.[11] Development is growth directed toward the production of an organism in accordance with a predetermined design. What exists at the start is only the design. This design includes an organizing and integrative principle that determines the course of growth and maintains the unity of the organism throughout the growth process. It does not include the form the organism will take. To create this form requires qualitative, as well as quantitative, transformations of the original, and hence an interaction with the environment. Furthermore, it involves an anticipation of future needs. That is, there exist potentialities for the formation of special behavior patterns related to future functions that may or may not be realized. An example is the impressive development of the embryo from conception to birth. During a relatively short period of time, an infinitesimal cell becomes a being capable of a totally different form of life. To talk in extremes, if one used the term growth for this process, one would be reverting to the preformation theories adhered to before the onset of embryology; if one used it for postnatal development, one would be reverting to the theories of faculty-psychology. Of course, nobody would do this today. However, the idea that developmental and maturational aspects of behavior are predetermined, and therefore exclusively the result of the growth process, is widespread. The counterpart of this idea is that the aspect of behavior complete in the embryonic stage, man accomplishes in his postnatal conditioning and instruction. The two scientists mentioned above,

Bruner and Coghill, have now accepted the fact that the creative process comes into play in growth and learning. They were reluctant to do so, however, and only the evidence obtained from their own investigations convinced them it was necessary.

Montessori's insight in this connection is quite fundamental and indeed simple. At birth man is relatively immature compared with other primates. This is a statement of fact. Consequently, part of the process of growth and development that these animals complete in the embryonic stage, man accomplishes in his postnatal state, when he is exposed to influences from the outside world. This is what Montessori means when she refers to the double embryonic life of the human species. She sees this further development as a continuation of the embryonic process, during which the individual actively participates in the process and it is related to the outer environment. It is therefore a psychological order. The postnatal stage is a formative period of intense activity during which the child must create in himself the basic structure of his personality. Nothing is preestablished. The child has only the potentialities needed to give form and content to his psychic life and, subsequently, to construct the basic patterns of behavior necessary to function independently in his environment.

The fact that this stage of development is still so little understood is, in my opinion, a paramount obstacle to the progress of the behavioral sciences. Biological evidence corroborating this principle in embryonic life was produced in 1940 by Coghill. Maria Montessori attached much importance to it. It seemed as if Coghill had reached conclusions similar to hers when he wrote, "Man is, indeed, a mechanism, but he is a mechanism which, within his limitations of life, sensitivity, and growth, is creating and operating himself." [12]

Because of his relative freedom from heredity, man must create within himself the organizing principle for directing his behavior. In a profound and detailed study of this subject, Dr. André Berge explains how man can only find his way in a world that he can conceive of as structured, physically as well as psychically. Man spontaneously classifies chaos according to a certain order. He can eventually replace this order with another order, but he cannot do without some kind of order. Dr. Berge sees in man's basic need for order the universal root of the moral phenomenon, a phenomenon that initially appears as an organizing principle. It is eventually incarnated in the moral apparatus of man and permits us to exist with a minimum of damage to others and to ourselves. It can, moreover, be the source of a special kind of pleasure: that of doing what we believe to be right. Hence, morality is not simply an internalized penal code. The great motor of our moral apparatus is love. This love is shifted, more or less, from the senses to the spirit; but it is nonetheless the same force that takes an individual out of himself and toward something for which he is capable of forgetting personal interests.[13]

The acquisition by an infant of its mother tongue is the best demonstration of that special quality of the child in the first years of life that Montessori calls the absorbent mind. "A special mechanism exists for language," she writes. "Not the possession of language in itself, but the possession of this mechanism which enables men to make languages of their own, is what distinguishes the human species." [14] Every normal child is able to speak its native tongue at the age of four. The actual language is dependent on the environment of the child, and there are individual differences in the moment the first intentional words are spoken and in subsequent progress and accuracy. However, the characteristic ability of an infant to master a language in this intensive way is universal. An adult no longer possesses this ability. Phenomenologically, there is an essential difference between the infant's conquest of its mother tongue and an adult's learning of a new language, which entails effort and determination. An infant learns a language playfully, and it becomes part of him. This miracle can only be achieved through some inner urge—a special sensitivity and a heightened direction of activity.[15]

The embryonic state of the human infant lasts approximately three years. At this time the human personality reaches a first level of integration. In the next three years a conscious elaboration and enrichment of what has been acquired unconsciously takes place. The type of mind is the same, but the child is more susceptible to adult influence with regard to learning. In the first period this influence is mainly the result of unconscious mechanisms determined by the emotional development of the child, which, in turn, is dependent on the child's close relationship with the adults who care for it. Introjection, imitation, and identification are of particular importance in the formation of behavior patterns and the acquisition of cultural attitudes.

In the second period this continues, but adults are now consciously acknowledged by the child as the source of information on social and cultural aspects of its existence. Because of its growing interest in these, the child turns spontaneously to adults with its queries. If it is not rejected, it responds with feelings of gratitude, trust, and respect for these superior beings who are willing to help it orient itself in its world. Its development continues to be guided from within by sensitive periods—time spans in which the child is sensitive to an incredible degree to a particular activity or interest. Discovered by Montessori in the early part of the century, these sensitive periods were completely ignored by academic psychologists until the late 1960s, when it was noted that modern research on the acquisition of linguistic skills had introduced the concept to account for data that could not otherwise be explained.[16]

Sensitive periods occur throughout the whole period of youth. This process is so long in man simply because all aspects of his personality must be formed by his own experiences as he interacts with the environment within a given community. The process of growth, maturation, and individuation, the result of the actualization of individual potentialities, is slow. These potentialities must be adapted and internalized in accordance with the developmental pattern typical of the human species. This cannot be achieved without the help of adults, help which is only available if love is the binding force in their relationship with the child.

Work is often considered as something forced on human beings by circumstances. Many forms of work in modern society certainly confirm this view. It may also have been applicable when self preservation inevitably involved work. However, work is also linked with man's creativity and is a universal phenomenon characteristic of the human species. One of Montessori's discoveries was that there are potentialities in the human personality that correspond to all such universal phenomena, directing the growing individual to perform specific activities. The experiences that result from these activities are needed to prepare him to perform functions that will be relevant at a later level of integration. This principle of indirect preparation is an essential feature of development. It is indirect preparation that eventually enables an individual to participate as an independent adult in those activities typical of the human species. The earliest roots of development are formed in the first years of life. These are the most important because, like language, they become part of the child. Since these developmental processes are unconscious, it is difficult to change them once the personality has been consolidated at the end of the first formative period, at about six years of age, and even more difficult after puberty.

The impact of early experiences with regard to emotional development has been fully confirmed by psychoanalytic studies. It is Montessori's achievement to have created conditions that permitted children to manifest their natural developmental propensities as part of ongoing working behavior. She gave children an appropriate environment and guided freedom within it so that they could act according to their inner needs, rhythm, and tempo, and as a result, they exhibited characteristics not generally attributed to them. These included deep and prolonged concentration, the repetition of exercises for their own sake, an urge to make a maximum effort, control of movements, a sense of order, and other phenomena. Perhaps the most astounding result of her approach was the intensity with which children approached activities. Their whole personalities were involved in them, and it was obvious that they were finding in their experiences the kind of pleasure and satisfaction that only results when basic needs are gratified. The aim of these activities was not to be found in the outer world, but within the children. They were forming their own personalities, constructing the men and women they were one day to become. Even after a forceful international campaign by Montessori for half a century, this difference in the aim of children's activities and adults' activities is still generally disregarded. Children's activities are still evaluated primarily from an adult point of view. Even those dedicated to the study of developmental psychology cannot sufficiently free themselves from the ingrained idea that a child is an inferior being. Therefore, they cannot discern the characteristics that can easily be observed when one is able to approach the child as a human being in his own right.

It is clear from an analysis of human development that education is an indispensable function in the formation of man. Montessori has pointed out that man's present predicament is caused by the lack of balance between him and his environment.[17] Education is the only means whereby we can hope to alter this situation. However, education can only help if it is reformed, if it is based on a better understanding of the human being, and, in particular, of the function of the child with regard to the formation of the human personality.

The panoramic view of Maria Montessori's fundamental and original contribution to human knowledge that I have tried to give in this chapter necessarily leaves out a wealth of detail and perhaps crowds too many ideas into a few pages. I hope, however, that it will serve as a base for the succeeding chapters, which deal in more detail with the relationship between Montessori and the sciences, the Montessori approach to work, and Montessori and traditional education. Chapter 2 is devoted to the Montessori materials, in particular their psychological background and their role in the social development of the child. It also attempts to clarify Montessori's position on play, which is so often misunderstood. Later chapters treat the role of education in today's world and the contemporary revolution in values as it relates to Montessori education.

NOTES

1. Günter Schulz-Benesch, "Montessori," in *Wege der Forschung,* vol. XX (Darmstadt: Wissenschaftliche Buchgesellschaft, 1970).

2. N. Perquin, S.J., in *Op zoek naar een pedagogisch denken,* J. J. Romen, ed. (Hoogveld Institute).

3. In psychology, a growing discontent with behaviorism, learning theory, and neopositivism is leading to a more human approach. See, for example, C. Kluckhohn, *Mirror for Man* (New York: McGraw-Hill, 1949), and F. E. Emery and E. L. Trist, *Towards a Social Ecology: Contextual Appreciation of the Future in the Present* (New York: Plenum, 1973).

4. Maria Montessori, *The Meaning of Adaptation* (Amsterdam: A.M.I. Communications, 1961).

5. Maria Montessori, *The Child in the Family* (Chicago: Regnery, 1970), pp. 112-13.

6. Maria Montessori, *Contributo clinico allo studio delle allucinazioni a contenuto antagonistico* (Rome, 1896).

7. Maria Montessori, *The Absorbent Mind* (New York: Holt, Rinehart and Winston, 1967) pp. 60-61.

8. Desmond Morris, *The Naked Ape* (New York: McGraw-Hill, 1968).

9. G. E. Coghill, *Anatomy and the Problem of Behavior* (New York and London: Hafner, 1964).

10. Jerome S. Bruner, *Toward a Theory of Instruction* (Cambridge, Mass.: Harvard University Press, 1966).

11. Alexis Carrel, *Man, the Unknown*, rev. ed. (New York: Harper & Brothers, 1939).

12. Coghill, p. 110.

13. André Berge, *Les maladies de la vertue* (Paris: Petite Bibliothèque Payot, 1960), pp. 31-40.

14. Montessori, *The Absorbent Mind*, p. 37.

15. With regard to the acquisition of language I particularly wish to recommend Eric H. Lenneberg's *Biological Foundations of Language*, with appendices by Noam Chomsky and Otto Marx (New York: Wiley, 1967). It is a challenging, original, erudite study that corroborates many of Maria Montessori's views on this subject with a wealth of evidence and offers ample opportunity for a scientific discussion of others.

16. H. C. J. Duyker and R. Vuyk, *Leerboek der Psychologie* (Groningen, Netherlands: Wolters-Noordhoof, 1969), p. 281, "gevoelige periode."

17. Maria Montessori, *The Formation of Man* (Adyar, India: Kalakshetra, 1955), pp. 14-17.

2 / THE MONTESSORI MATERIALS: *Their Function and Relationship to the Child's Work, Play, and Social Life*

Montessori saw education as a means whereby children might develop their personalities so as to eventually achieve a mature and independent adulthood. She designed her educational material to aid them in this endeavor. This fundamental function of the material is generally disregarded when it is compared with the equipment found in most preprimary classrooms. Disappointment with the Montessori material results because the comparisons that are made are only superficial. This superficial approach is encouraged by adherence to either of the two main trends of current thought in education. One of these holds that young children should be free to express their urges and fantasies without restraint, thus experiencing a minimum of frustration. Objects should mainly serve to offer possibilities of gratification. In handling them, the children will also discover some of their objective qualities, but this is more or less a side issue. Learning at this early stage is held to hamper the uninhibited development of the child's personality, and therefore to be something that should not be enforced by organized teaching. From this point of view, the Montessori material appears too rigid.

The second approach to education popular today considers all development an integral part of the learning process, and all learning to be the result of conditioning, deconditioning, or reconditioning originally simple reflexes. Knowledge can therefore be gained from experiments with rats and other animals, and then applied to human beings in a learning situation. Although the human organism achieves a higher level of differentiation, the chains of reactions encountered basically correspond to the same mechanical model. Whatever new theoretical constructs may be envisaged must obey the laws inherent in this basic theory. This is considered to be true even before the switch to the experimentation and observation of humans is made. Any imaginable skill within the abilities of the nervous system at a given stage of maturation can thus be acquired by the individual, providing an appropriate conditioning based on the accepted theoretical laws can be undertaken. Those accepting this view will find the Montessori material lacking in detailed systemization; for instance, in the programming of instructions. They will, therefore, consider it too limited in scope for proper learning.

This is an incomplete and oversimplified exposition of two widely accepted approaches in education, but I hope it will serve to make my point concerning Montessori education clear. It does include the more fundamental viewpoints of these schools of thought. However, they are seen only as parts of the basic educational pattern, a pattern that is derived from a broader conception of human development. The discussion above also illustrates an important point concerning education in general. Whether it is being explicitly postulated or not, the aims of education and the methods used to achieve these aims are determined by the psychological matrix resulting from the underlying general conception of human development.

Montessori actually presents a third, more comprehensive conception of education. As I have mentioned, she sees a basic biological difference between men and animals. This difference is clearly visible in the patterns underlying the behavior of individual human beings, which are not predominantly determined by heredity. Man must build these inner structures from which he evolves his personal behavior during his lifetime, and from his own experiences. In animals, instinct predominates and other functions are subordinate. An animal's general behavior and the relation of its species to its specific environment are included in the pattern of instinct with which it is born, and are therefore hereditary. In man, that which corresponds to this aspect of the animal instinct materializes only after birth. It is an inner creation accomplished by man in the course of his youth, which is more protracted than that of any other living being. This creation takes place in a relationship of dependence on the community in which the individual develops, and from which he cannot be considered a separate entity.

However, this does not imply that man is a product of his environment, or that his development is left to chance. It is, rather, a complex process directed by inner drives that succeed one another at certain periods in his life. These drives are closely interrelated with the sequences of maturation and development, as well as with outer reality. These inner directives, however, are of a different order than animal instincts. Montessori called them "guiding instincts." They indicate the route man's mental development will take. Because this development can only take place within society, the cultural values of the time will help define its form.

Inner development must precede independence. Therefore, it is this inner development that is the child's major task. To accomplish it, the child is equipped with certain potentialities that do not exist, as such, in adults. One of these Montessori called "the absorbent mind." Through their close emotional ties with those who take care of them, children actively absorb, during the first years of life, the basic patterns they encounter in their social environment. From these their personal behavior will take shape. This pronounced sensitivity to and eagerness to assimilate impressions from the outside exists not only in relation to other living beings and their behavior, but encompasses everything that goes to make up the child's world. His emotional relationship with the external world is so intense that it strongly influences his whole being. This is why Montessori has called the child in this phase of development the "spiritual embryo." In later stages of development, children are led toward maturity by "sensitive periods" that stimulate them to carry out certain activities and to acquire certain experiences. These are necessary for the further structuring of their own personalities in relation to their environment. The possibilities offered by the surrounding world determine whether this predisposition toward new experiences with their resulting enrichment of the personality, is fully stimulated, merely used in part, or even quenched.

According to Montessori, education should be an aid to life.

Therefore, it must be an instrument for the support and guidance of the child in the monumental task of constructing the foundation of his personality. Three factors determine the course of this inner construction. The first is the child's own psyche, with its specific needs, potentialities, and sensitive periods, which determines the pace and direction of its inner development. This development does not occur in straight lines, but shows fluctuations and individual differences. The second is the cultural community, with its standards, habits, patterns of behavior, ideals, religion, and knowledge of all other aspects of its civilization. It is the prevailing order of this community that permits the child to achieve an inner harmony. The third is the material world with all its objective qualities, to which man must adapt himself in order to be able to utilize his own faculties freely.

The environment of modern man is highly differentiated and complex. A being confronted for the first time by the present world could not help but feel confused. Yet a child, once it has left the confinement of its mother's womb, must eventually come to terms with this world. It can only do this through experiences. Adults must give it the freedom to gain this experience in its own way. At the same time, they must help it, when possible, to explore and assimilate its world and the principles prevailing in it. They must, therefore, construct a bridge between their world and that of the child. Montessori education provides this bridge through the prepared environment. It is here that the Montessori material plays a fundamental role. The idea is not to reproduce the adult world in miniature, or to distort reality into a make-believe paradise in which children's wishes and fantasies are the only things considered. Rather, the prepared environment should bring the world at large, and thus the adult world, within reach of the child at whatever stage of development it is at a given moment.

In order to achieve this, the prepared environment should meet certain general requirements. First, it should be attractive, aesthetically and practically, from the standpoint of children of different age groups, but reflect that amount of organization and order necessary for a community to function properly. The rules used to achieve this should be valid for all. They ought to be derived not from the adult's wish to impose his authority, but, as in regulating traffic, from a desire to allow every individual freedom of independent activity as long as his freedom does not interfere with that of others. The prepared environment should also stimulate the interest of the children in the kind of purposeful activities they need to further their general development. It must also be so arranged that they can carry out these activities in their own way and at their own rate. The environment should not be centered on a single function or skill, but call to a child's whole personality. Moreover, there should be ample opportunity in the environment for the child to practice, work through, and integrate with previous skills any new function or skill that has been acquired. This should also be true with regard to general behavior. Children should feel comfortable in the prepared environment. Their limitations as well as their possibilities should be taken into consideration in creating it. It should be made to measure for them so that they have the opportunity to behave independently whenever they have learned to do so. Adults should guide and help the child when necessary, but not unnecessarily. If, for example, toilet training has been successful and children can be independent in this regard, they should not have to ask the aid of an adult just because the utilities available are too big for them. These should be adapted to the children's smaller stature. So should the furniture and any other objects in the environment that are there for their use. If the environment is not so arranged, the children are constantly confronted with tasks which they see adults perform and which they know they could do also, if they were not too small in relation to the objects involved. They may come to regard adults, therefore, as powerful rivals instead of models. Finally, the prepared environment should contain material purposely constructed and selected to provide the children with the means of having certain basic experiences pertinent to their development. The Montessori material is not purely didactic, nor does it consist of toys, although the children learn from it and play with it, and, what is more, love doing so.

The Montessori material is only one of several devices by which the Montessori principles find expression. Now that its position has been established within the general frame of reference of the other two approaches to education, we can consider its special function.

When used properly, this material serves two main purposes. On the one hand, it furthers the inner development of the child: specifically, the indirect preparation that must precede the development of any new ego function. On the other, it helps the child to acquire new perspectives in its exploration of the objective world. It makes it aware of certain qualities of the objects, their interrelationships, existing principles of differentiation within a given category, organizational sequences, and special techniques for handling the objects. It challenges the intelligence of the child, who is first intrigued and later fully absorbed by the principles involved. If a spark is lit, a principle discovered, it awakens in the child an urge to exercise its newly acquired insight through endless repetitions of the action that led to it. When the child has fully mastered the principle involved, it spontaneously proceeds to apply it in handling all kinds of objects. The material does not, in the first place, teach children factual knowledge. Instead it makes it possible for them to reorganize their knowledge according to new principles. This increases their capacity for learning. Because the material serves this function, Montessori referred to it as materialized abstractions.

I should like to illustrate these two main aspects of the material with some examples. All ego functions, like perception, thinking, language, the comprehension of objects, and the coordination of movements and learning processes in general, require a long period of indirect preparation before they emerge as integrated aspects of the personality. This results in certain activities on the part of children which make no sense to adults. Often, children abandon themselves to these activities with such tenacity that it is very difficult to distract them.

I once witnessed the following scene. A small girl who was not yet able to walk, but who could move around quite adequately, pulled herself up by gripping the side of the living room coffee table. She then began to investigate a little vase of flowers on top of it. She held herself upright, supporting herself by putting her left hand on the table, and started to pull the flowers, one by one, out of the vase with her right hand, putting them on the table. While thus engaged, she exhibited all the seriousness and concentration one expects from a surgeon in an operating theater. The water on the doily did not disturb her, nor did her mother, who enjoyed looking at this performance because of the intensity of purpose it expressed. As soon as all the flowers were on the table, the little girl started putting them back in the vase, one by one, with the greatest care. When she was finished she commenced to remove them again. This had been going on for some time when I entered the room. The little girl disregarded my entrance completely. She was on her fifth or sixth round and had no intention of stopping. It was as if the rest of the world did not exist for her. The mother and I kept watching her, fascinated. However, it was lunch time, and rather late at that, so after a while, when all the flowers were once more in the vase, the mother suggested going to lunch. Her daughter paid no attention whatsoever, and started again with a new round. The mother, although appreciating the fact that this activity seemed important to the child, did not want to have her or the rest of the family miss lunch, so she continued with her summons in a friendly, but persistent, manner. Finally, the child, without looking up or interrupting what she was doing, said with some vehemence "No, no!", and went on. At this point the flowers were again on the table, and the mother said, "Well, just put them back in the vase, but then we shall have lunch." The child said "No!" again and went on until the flowers were all back in place, only to start the proceedings all over again. This time her mother was firm in her intention and took her daughter up smilingly, promising her nice food and permission to continue with the flowers after lunch. The child was simply desperate, wailing and crying big tears, even when she was sitting in front of her food. It took quite a lot of cuddling and comforting before she calmed down. Happily, she was hungry, so that once she had detached her attention from her previous activity and her fit had passed, the alternative of eating was also attractive and she could again smile at the world.

This example is typical of the sort of activity that, to superficial observers, seems quite superfluous, especially if they judge it by adult standards. What is the use of putting flowers in and out of a vase endlessly? Still, for a child, it can be a very serious matter. The purpose of the activity, however, must be sought within the child, and not in the action itself or its objective aim.

The other function of the Montessori material, to help children acquire new perspectives, is illustrated by the following experience I had with a girl four years old. We were sitting on a large couch with a cretonne covering that she had crawled and jumped on a great deal throughout her short life, as it was just under a window looking out on the street. We were chatting a bit in a gay mood. All of a sudden she lost interest in me, and looking quite seriously at the cushion on which we were sitting, said nothing for a while. I was wondering what might have caught her attention when she pointed with her small finger at a spot of the decoration in the flowery cretonne and said, "This is dark green." A little while later, pointing to another spot, she added, "And this is lighter green." She then found a still lighter spot and said, "This is the lightest." When the green shades were exhausted, she started examining another color, then another, and so on. I then joined her, following her statements with questions about other shades, and we continued until I had to go. Now, the interesting part of this story is that what the little girl learned with the Montessori material was not the colors themselves, nor their names, which she already knew. It was the concept of shades, which enabled her to rediscover this piece of furniture she had been so accustomed to all her life. She was looking at her own world with other eyes, as it were, and with a more differentiated perception.

These effects can only be expected when the material offered to a child corresponds to the kind of activities in which it has a special interest at that stage, and when its intelligence is sufficiently developed for it to grasp the idea involved. If material is given to a child too soon, it seems too difficult; if too late, it is boring. If, however, the time is right, it will be experienced as something the child can conquer. Montessori material offers children symbols and a means of interpreting their world in a more coherent and differentiated way. It therefore stimulates their wish to learn by making learning neither frustrating nor burdensome, but pleasurable.

Whoever has seen a Montessori child at the moment in its life when it discovers that it can read will never forget its happiness, its beaming face, its pride that a new world has been opened to it. I have had this privilege with my own children, and it has convinced me that something very fundamental and constructive happens to children in Montessori schools. No matter what theories are involved, I should not wish to have deprived any of my children of this unique experience. It has also brought something new to our relationship. The children now not only have the joy of reading and making sense out of formerly mysterious symbols, but they also experience the joy of sharing something with adults, something which until that moment belonged exclusively to the latter's world. Now the children have entered this world as well. They have something new in common with the parents with whom they identify. The bond between them has been strengthened and made more realistic, and the children's still weak egos have been strengthened too. All this has come about in a miraculous way without the children knowing that it would happen. It is this element of discovery that makes the Montessori approach to reading a unique and gratifying experience.

The Montessori materials are generally used individually in the classroom. Therefore, it is important to consider whether a method that emphasizes their use can do justice to the social needs of children.

Historically, the Montessori method has been called an individual approach, to differentiate it from the classical approach, the only method in use in schools in the early part of the century. The fact is, however, that social education has always had an important place in Montessori schools. A number of factors contribute to this education: the role of the teacher, the free method of work, the prepared environment—which encourages respect for others and for materials—and the inclusion of children of varying ages in one group.

Montessori described the adult's function in the classroom as one of guiding in contrast to teaching. In fact, she discarded the term teacher altogether, preferring that of directress. Without guidance, no single community can come into being. Somebody must see to the maintenance of the patterns of behavior that are deemed necessary for ordered coexistence within a given group. Although the school community bears some resemblance to the family, it also differs from it, and therefore demands further social growth. Teachers are the representatives of this wider community. They must help the children by gradually familiarizing them with its rules. Furthermore, this must be done in a manner that makes their inner acceptance by the children possible.

Teachers must uphold the rules of the school community for the benefit of the group as well as that of individual children. Accordingly the only punishment in Montessori education is isolation from the group for a temporary period. If a child behaves in a way that disturbs others, the teacher explains to him that others cannot continue their activities. She suggests that they go and look for something he would like to do. If he continues to be disruptive, he is set apart with his table, chair, and material. He can still see the group, but he is isolated from it. However, he is free to rejoin the others when he thinks that he is once more able to participate. It is the social situation that determines when such measures are necessary, and it is the child's positive desire to belong that motivates him to correct his behavior.

The balance between freedom for the individual and the needs of the group is another special feature of social education in the Montessori method. One can only speak of a true community when each member of the group feels sufficiently free to be himself or herself, while simultaneously restricting his or her own freedom for the sake of adjustment to the group. It is in seeking an optimal solution to this tension between personal independence and dependence on the group that the social being is formed. Too much individual freedom leads to chaos. Too much uniformity, imposed by adults, leads to impersonal conformity or to rebellion.

The prepared environment encourages social development by making it necessary for the children to consider both objects and others. Because the environment is adapted to their inner needs, it is attractive and stimulating to them. It invites them to engage in all kinds of activity. There are certain restrictions on this activity, however. First of all, the materials impose certain conditions. Controls of error are built into them. Whenever these conditions are not satisfied the objects themselves confront the children with their properties. The children are thus presented with problems for which they must seek better solutions if they wish to fulfill the tasks they have chosen to perform. This factual relation to the objects promotes inner adjustment to their environment.

Similarly, an outward adjustment is also required, for everything in the prepared environment has its own special location. After material has been used, it must be returned to its original place and condition so that other children can work with it or, not finding it, can know that it is already in use. This outward adjustment is achieved through following the instructions of the teacher, through the children's awareness of the needs of others, and through the order of the environment itself, which arouses the children's desire to collaborate in maintaining it. These forms of adjustment are important aspects of the process of adaptation that determines the social development of the individual.

Respect for others is further developed through the children's relationship with the teacher in the prepared environment. When a child first comes to school at the age of two and a half or three, it has little direct contact with other children. This is because emotionally the young child turns much more to the adults in its surroundings. It develops a personal tie first with its mother, then with its father, and then with other trusted adults in its first milieu. A tie with its teacher becomes a further extension of this sequence. Teachers occupy just as important a place in a class as a child's mother does at home, and children turn naturally to them for help. The relationship that develops is less personal than the mother–child relationship, but a positive tie between teacher and child is the only satisfactory basis for education. For this reason Montessori called education a technique of love.

Teachers must actively strive to establish a positive relationship so that children will approach them with confidence and accept their authority as a matter of course. In order to do this, they should make themselves as attractive as they can, not only in appearance but as a source of new, happy experiences. They must respect the children's personalities, understand their developmental needs, and appreciate their achievements. In this way, they avoid standing opposite the children as a representative of arbitrary authority and take their place beside them as wiser persons who understand them and who are willing to help them in their endeavors to grow toward adulthood. The children in turn respond with affection and a willingness to accept the teachers' guidance.

Once this type of relationship has been established, they can gradually help the children to become members of the class community, something that is only possible when they respect the interests of the group and help to maintain the existing social order. They learn to use the material with care so that it remains in good condition for the use of others, to assist in keeping the mutually shared environment attractive and orderly, to behave in such a way that others can work undisturbed, to develop good manners that make them at ease in various social situations, and to postpone the satisfaction of their own wishes when they conflict with the demands of reality and the needs of others. All this is done in as natural a way as possible whenever the occasion arises.

Montessori was one of the first to realize how important collective work is for mental development. Therefore, she strove to create optimal conditions for its realization in her schools. The exercises of practical life for the young children promote social contact both because of the nature of the task and because of the way in which they are organized in the classroom. It is a common sight to see little groups of two or more children who have voluntarily begun to do these exercises together. Collective work continues to be emphasized in Montessori education all through preprimary and secondary education. At the beginning of a working period, a short lesson is given on a general subject that may interest the whole group. When this proves a success, it often results in a wave of activity among the children. Sometimes this results in their working together directly. At other times they may work individually, on their own level and according to their own insight and abilities. However, they are at the same time taking part in a group event, for their separate contributions are on a common subject and can later be seen by everyone as a collective achievement. There are, of course, class discussions when, for example, on a Monday morning the teacher gives the children the opportunity to tell about their weekend experiences. In this way they learn to speak before a group, to give each other a chance to speak, and to make relevant contributions to a line of thought. At the same time they hear about one another's daily life. Especially after a vacation, this gives rise to compositions and drawings based on their experiences. In addition, the children often react actively to things the teacher reads to them, what the teacher says to them about a subject that everyone in the adult world is discussing, in the preparation of a science display, and so on. There are also individual activities in the service of the group, such as the care of the plants and animals in the classroom, the cleaning of the shelves and materials, and the distribution of food for snacks. There are group activities such as making decorations for the classroom for festive days and celebrations, the silence lesson, exercises on the line, dancing, and singing. Plays and dialogues are created, and there are indoor and outdoor games of all sorts. In short, a good Montessori classroom will be the scene of a variety of collective activities.

It remains now to consider whether the individual emphasis of the Montessori materials is suitable for young children, for it is indeed true that children who are working with the materials are quietly doing so on their own. In psychological literature this solitary type of occupation is generally labeled egocentric. In my opinion, this term is only correct if the behavior of the child is judged by adult standards. This, of course, is what the psychologists in question actually do. If, however, one takes account of the child's own nature, it is immediately clear that this term cannot be used to describe its activity. A small child is capable of becoming wholly absorbed and fascinated by what it is doing. But it is occupied with the materials on which it is concentrating, and not with itself.

Of course, children in a Montessori class do much more than work with the material. They are well aware of those around them, and one often sees the small ones watching the work of others, particularly the older ones, intensely. In doing this they absorb much more than it seems, and are already preparing themselves for more active social participation in the community of the class. The contribution of the Montessori classroom to the development of a social life sometimes goes unnoticed because of the emphasis on the inner growth of the child. Often one thinks of social development in terms of mutual contact. This is to underestimate the process involved. A long period of indirect preparation is indispensable if a child is to develop the capacity of relating to others. As in all areas of human development, nothing is achieved immediately and rectilinearly.

Children quietly practicing on their own with Montessori

materials are unconsciously preparing themselves for participation in the community in which they will later have to find their places as independent adults. The Montessori method is specifically designed to aid them in this important task. If there are Montessori teachers who have not grasped this goal of education, to which the method owes its highly dynamic character, it is due to their own limitations, and not to the method itself. Any teacher or other adult who fails to appreciate the importance of this inner development devalues man to the level of a gregarious animal and denies the child the help it needs to become truly what it is intended to be: a social being.

I would like now to discuss a third area related to the Montessori materials, that of play, because it has always been—and still is—surrounded by misunderstanding and criticism. In the course of time, however, the direction of critical comment has shifted. Where formerly it was held that children in Montessori schools could do what they liked, and thus played all day long, today the reverse is contended. It is said that the children may only do what Maria Montessori wanted them to do, so that their need for free play is not satisfied.

In order to see Montessori's view of play in proper perspective, it is necessary to recognize the historical context in which she began her work. First of all, schools for children under the age of five or six were the exception rather than the rule. In cases where separate facilities could be provided for very young children, they were nursery facilities where toys were played with under the watchful eye of a governess and where they were more or less left to their own devices.

Since young children were not deemed capable of anything but play, they were given only those objects which, in the opinion of adults, seemed most suitable for this typical and rather senseless form of behavior. The toys that could be bought were generally pretty and ingenious, but they were not sufficiently adapted to the children's own nature. Their design was mainly determined by what attracted adults. They were therefore based on a projection of adult likes onto children, and not on what children themselves needed to play with. The practice of giving toys to children implied a sense of superiority on the part of adults, who did not take the children's play seriously, but merely wanted to please them. It reminds one of the behavior of the white traders who offered hand mirrors and colored glass beads to the chiefs of primitive tribes to establish good trade relations. Children's play was regarded by adults more as a childish business than as fundamental human behavior at an early stage of development. Only when a child did something that fitted adult expectations, that is, when it was being least a child, could it expect appreciation.

Montessori, however, wanted to study children in their own world. Therefore, in seeking the optimum conditions for her scientific experiment, she let herself be guided by the spontaneous activity, reactions, and expressions of children. She started by offering them all the usual toys that were supposed to please them; but she also introduced new ones, some of which were the same as the materials found in Montessori schools today. From the children's point of view, they simply continued playing, but with more intriguing playthings. For the observer, however, revelations of lasting importance resulted. The exteriorizing of the contents of the child's own experience by creating shapes out of formless material, the elaboration of impressions from daily life by acting them out alone or with other children, the expression of dominating emotions through fantasies of all kinds, and inexhaustible physical activity were the accepted forms of typical childlike behavior throughout the ages, although they were never completely understood. The new aspects of child behavior that came to light through Montessori's work clearly demonstrated for the first time that children have an inner need to learn to know themselves and their world: to develop their intelligence and other mental functions through purposeful activity, to develop control of their movements through the use of their bodies in specific structured situations, to organize the contents of their experience according to the order they encounter in the world, and, finally, through an acquaintance with the properties of things, to grow familiar with their environment and with their own capacities in order, eventually, to become independent.

All this happens in a manner natural to children and of their own volition, and therefore should be termed play. Yet, when children are adequately aided in this respect, one is struck by the new qualities they develop: the maximum effort very young children put forth, the repetition of exercises time and again—not for the sake of the end result—but for the sake of the activity itself, the sense of order, the intensive concentration once a task has aroused a child's interest, the joy in work, the growing self-confidence and social ease, and all the other manifestations that inspired Montessori to develop her educational method.

Two main attitudes can be distinguished in the spontaneous behavior of children. The first is a desire for self-expression. The direction of events is, as it were, from the inside to the outside. Objects serve as a means to express the contents of a child's own experience, its capacities, and the products of its fantasy. That which lives in the child itself is exteriorized by its use of objects and the meaning it gives them in free play.

The less structured objects are and the more they function merely as raw materials, the more appropriate they are for this purpose. Clay, sand, water, beads, coloring materials, blank paper, art materials of many kinds, can serve very well in this connection. A boy running with a stick between his legs and acting out the fantasy that he is a mighty cowboy on horseback chasing a group of Indians singlehandedly, would not benefit from being given a real horse, or a toy horse, in exchange for his stick. The stick does not even function as a symbol of a horse. It is actually no more than a sign: a sign that indicates the transition between reality and fantasy and also maintains the connection between the two. It is similar to the signposts in medieval theater that indicated the scenario, which the stage setting itself left to the imagination of the spectators.

When children, either alone or with others, are busy with such fantasy play, adults can offer them little help. The usefulness of objects is also limited, for they must fit, or be made by the children to fit, into the fantasy world. The children alone know how that world has to be organized and what significance to assign to the objects. The objects should lend a quality of reality to the children's fantasy without disturbing its free course by having too specific properties or by being too differentiated. In all fantasies, especially those with an emotional content, a child is confronted with its personal experience. They enable it to achieve a conscious elaboration of this experience. On the other hand, the child gets none the wiser about the world's objective qualities, the properties of things and their interrelations, or the organization of its environment from a fantasy. Children themselves give form to their fantasies, and reality must comply with the dictates of imagination.

When reality does not support a child's fantasy, or when occurrences in the immediate environment or events connected with the child's own body claim its attention, the child's attitude toward the outer world changes. If, for instance, a screaming fire engine races past, the boy with the stick horse forgets for the moment to be a cowboy and turns with curiosity to that real occurrence. It is characteristic of such situations that children do not create their own world but are, as it were, drawn out of it by the call of reality and venture forth to meet the things that exist in the world in their own shape. Compliance must now come from the children's side if they want to get better acquainted with these real events and real things, and test them on their own merits. Things have their own significance and organization, their own characteristics, values, and possible uses. The world exhibits a definite structure in which various principles of order, laws, and mutual relations can be discerned. Objects in the world therefore make demands on the children's power of combination, on their insight, and on their ability to coordinate their movements. Unless these conditions are met, they cannot make adequate use of real world things that they encounter.

The form of inner construction taking place when children are engaged in fantasy play, or whether any kind of self-construction at all is occurring, is not known. However, as a spontaneous form of activity in children, fantasy play deserves serious study. Montessori did find that, given a choice, children chose the activities that eventually came to compose the Montessori environment. She herself made no value judgment about this choice. She merely observed it, and accepted the children's behavior. The fact that Montessori children generally chose activities that informed them about the world outside themselves, may be in part the result of two aspects of their lives. First, the practical life activities, based as they are on actions the children see adults performing in their environment, may partially meet their need for dramatic play (which seems to be based on copying what they see about them).[1] Second, children in our culture tend to have more opportunities for self-expressive play than for activities that develop their knowledge of the outer world. Therefore, given a choice, they tend to choose the latter.

In this chapter, I have discussed the role of the Montessori materials in some detail: their primary role as an indirect preparation for ego functions and the differentiation of the child's intelligence; the position they hold in its developing social life; and their relationship to its needs both for self-expression, as in fantasy play, and for self-realization based on contact with outer reality. The role of the materials has been misunderstood by both admirers and critics, but it need not be. If one understands Montessori's basic approach to education as an aid to life, the role of the materials falls logically into place. They are, quite simply, aids to the child in its self-construction.

NOTE

1. Montessori's appreciation of drama in general is often forgotten. For very young children, she suggested such activities as extemporaneous acting inspired by a beginning sentence such as "Maria went to the window and cried. . . ." The older children in Montessori schools write and produce original plays. In some classrooms the afternoons are devoted almost exclusively to various kinds of artistic expression, including plays. The latter are often based on history or literature. For example, an original play may be put on depicting a historical period or event, with authentic costumes, props, and scenery. One school I visited (the Montessori School of Northern Virginia, 6820 Pacific Lane, Annandale, Virginia 22003) had been to a production of Shakespeare a few weeks earlier, and one of the children had asked to see the slides the teacher had taken during the performance. While the slides were being shown, several children spontaneously spoke the lines from the scenes being depicted. The play was *Midsummer Night's Dream,* and the entertainment superb as one nine-year-old boy in particular raised his voice to take the leading female role, acting the part to perfection.

3 / MONTESSORI EDUCATION AND MODERN PSYCHOLOGY

Since the Montessori method grew out of a scientific investigation, it seems appropriate to examine whether this method meets the demands that modern science, and psychology in particular, make on education. To do this, it is necessary to recount Montessori's view of man and the principles on which the rest of her work is based so that they can be compared with the findings of modern psychology.

Of course, the term "modern psychology" implies a unity of outlook that does not in fact exist. A certain amount of disunity, theoretical controversy, and mutual negative criticism has naturally resulted from the great expansion and progress that this young science has experienced within a short time. Furthermore, it is still far from reaching its final goal. Perhaps one reason for this is the fact that its object of study—human behavior—is so very complex. It is certainly more difficult for us to penetrate than something with which we are less directly involved. In spite of this, and notwithstanding the contradictory opinions held by individual psychologists, there is sufficient essential agreement on certain points for a general view of man to be outlined. Some of its fundamental characteristics are as follows:

- Man is, above all, a social being. That is, he is dependent on his social environment not only for his physical survival but for his psychic and spiritual development. Of all living creatures, he alone possesses language. Language is not the product and possession of an individual, but of society.

• Cultural heritages, which are inconceivable without society, give content and form to human existence; they indicate paths by which man can fulfill his particular destiny. Since this destiny is interpreted differently from culture to culture, human beings need each other to realize, collectively, the possibilities of humanity. The great human values, such as faith, justice, beauty, and truth, are created and supported by the community. Within it they have general validity as aims indissolubly related to human talent. They have a suprapersonal, supraindividual nature, and cannot, therefore, be understood or explained by looking at the individual.

• The individual is only potentially human. He is, as it were, a promise that can only be fulfilled by society. He is different, therefore, from an animal, which reaches the limits of its development soon after birth and may then be considered complete.

• The continuity in human history is a cultural continuity, whereas the continuity in the animal world is in principle biological. The fundamental psychosomatic unity is another principle that comes strongly to the fore in contemporary psychology.

• Man finds in his organism the source of his own activity. This he directs toward his environment, either strivingly or resistently, through his behavior.

• Behavior is the term used to describe the meaningful activity by which man enters into a relationship with his environment. Since he has alternatives in this regard, human behavior is the physical manifestation of a choice.

• Man's behavior is only partially determined by the laws of nature. Insofar as he has alternatives, he must make choices. He possesses the widest range of possible choices of all living beings because he is capable of creating alternatives that do not, as such, exist in nature. On the other hand, an alternative that was originally present may be lost, and then a pure automatism comes into function. Therefore all addiction and rigidity is, in a sense, a deficiency when measured by the yardstick of human possibilities.

- Behavior is always in reference to something and has meaning. The setting of and striving after aims is a fundamental aspect of human existence. Even before a child can speak, or for that matter before anyone can explain to it what an aim is, it already has aims. Because man experiences himself as the source of activity, he is also aware of intentionality. He has this awareness at an early age.
- Modern psychology begins with the conviction that human behavior is not purely accidental, but is determined by something. In other words, it occurs in a context of determinants.
- The totality of relationships from which man determines his behavior is called a situation. Man constantly finds himself in situations. As his development progresses, these situations become richer, and consequently his behavior becomes more differentiated. However, this differentiation varies from person to person according to the individual's interests, abilities, and circumstances.

How does this brief outline of man as he is presented to us in psychological literature today compare with the view of man Maria Montessori presents to us? Montessori held the following beliefs:

- Man appeared on the evolutionary scene as a new being. In spite of his biological resemblance to the higher animals, he is fundamentally different from them. This difference is not one of overall superiority. Man as an individual is weaker than many animals, and certainly weaker than those animal species presumed to have inhabited the earth when he first made his appearance. It is said that his weapon is intelligence. However, the intelligence of the individual means little when he lives in isolation.
- In animals, the ability to adapt is limited. Their consciousness is confined to their needs and the striving to satisfy them. They live in bondage to hereditary patterns of behavior from which they can deviate only slightly and then only in special circumstances. Man is different. He is far more flexible. He too possesses certain instincts, but they are less structured than those of animals and they do not determine the patterns of behavior that give form and content to his existence. He must construct these patterns himself, and he can only do this in assocation with his fellow men.

- Man cannot be understood as an individual. It is only in a community that he becomes human and that his potentialities can be realized.
- The animal biosphere has an organization that appears to be more or less static. Man has called into existence a psychosphere that is dynamic and changeable. Since his behavior is not determined hereditarily, he seeks self-realization. In the course of this search, he has learned to change his natural environment and has made discoveries that have gradually brought about the present state of civilization. What is generally referred to as our social environment—a milieu that in the course of history acquired its present form—is no longer natural, but is a supranatural creation.
- Work is inherent in human existence. Most people, therefore, work, and many discover new things; but individual discoveries only become valuable when they are accepted and applied by a larger group.
- However convinced someone may be that he is working only for himself, he is in fact working for the community; and only the results of this communal activity, which we call civilization, show continuity and progress.
- The link that makes this continuity possible is the child, with its specific potentialities.
- People do not unite by holding onto one another. Their hands must be free for the activity by which the individual tries to realize his own destiny. He does this independently, in accordance with his personal capacities and possibilities.
- The bond between human beings is their common intelligence, and language is the vehicle that makes the abstract intelligence of a community possible. It is only as a member of a group that the individual can accomplish his task as a human being. Yet man's existence within the group must also be safeguarded by agreement on the general rules of conduct, since patterns of behavior are not determined by natural laws.
- The higher values generally accepted by a community constitute the spiritual pole according to which the individual directs his striving toward self-realization and, in doing so, constantly sacrifices some of his self-interest. Their content and interpreta-

tion vary from culture to culture and also among the various groups within a greater community. But the need for religion and for norms is an essential characteristic of human nature.

• The conglomerate of spiritual and material values which we term civilization and which determines the cultural climate of a community is no static entity. It is constantly being added to and revised. The dominating patterns in it change and evolve in the course of time, affecting man's behavior.

The parallels between the two views of man presented here—that of Montessori and modern psychology—are certainly striking. Her personal contribution is her identification of children as the link that guarantees the continuity of human evolution, which is a cultural evolution. Because of their close emotional bond with those into whose care they are given, children turn, with their special sensibilities and potentialities, to adults. From them, they unconsciously absorb the fundamental patterns on which they base their personal behavior during their childhood. Their minds absorb and digest impressions of the social environment as they travel the road toward their own destiny in society.

A convincing example of the child's capabilities in this area is provided by Marie-Yvonne Vellard, a child of the Guayaki Indians, a South American tribe living a hidden, nomadic existence on the Stone Age level. In 1932 she was abandoned in the forest by two women of the tribe when they were surprised by members of an expedition led by Dr. Jean Albert Vellard, director of the French Institute of Indian Studies at Lima. She was adopted, and subsequently raised, by Dr. Vellard and has become an educated woman who speaks several languages and who, apart from her appearance, does not differ from the Latin American friends with whom she shared her upbringing. During a UNESCO conference in Paris on racial problems, her case was quoted as evidence that all men are equal at birth.[1] It took our ancestors two hundred centuries to go from the Stone Age to the Atomic Age. This girl did it in one leap. An adult member of her tribe, even the most intelligent, would not have been able to adapt to the modern world in this way. Some indication of what might have been achieved can be found in a touching human document relating the brief encounter with twentieth-century civilization of Ishi, the last survivor of a California Indian tribe. He emerged from the Stone Age into the modern world in 1911, and although intelligent and sensitive, his cultural being remained unchanged.[2] Only children possess the spiritual ability (the absorbent mind) necessary for the formation of the future man.

So far we have examined only Montessori's global view of man, and the principles on which she based her method. Although this view is in accordance with modern psychology, it does not follow that its practical applications are. A brief summary of Montessori's reasoning and that of psychology will indicate whether, in fact, they are. An analysis of the various trends and schools in psychology shows that there is agreement on several fundamental points, which consequently may be considered representative of modern psychology:

- A psychic event only acquires meaning when it is related to a higher totality, in the final analysis, to the personality as a whole.
- The relevant organizing principle is not the law, but the type. The total individual should be studied and his psychological structure compared with the psychological structures of other individuals so that its type can be determined.
- The organic totality of personality is directed toward the realization of certain aims and values. It is important to understand the internal striving of psychic life toward aims and to consider psychic activity from the viewpoint of finality.

- Phenomena and functions have meaning in the life of the individual, who is not a passive mechanism, but an active, striving being.
- The meaning of a phenomenon cannot be understood from studying the unrelated process alone, but only from examining the meaningful whole of which it forms a part.
- Man is a spiritual being and strives for certain cultural values.
- All psychological processes are related to the subject, which is active. The ego is the center that gives direction to these psychological processes.
- Not only the content of experience but the action function of the ego comes to the fore.

- Man's emotional and volitional life is important, as is his social aspect.
- The psychosomatic unity of man is fundamental.
- Behavior is the physical manifestation of a choice. It springs from an alternative.

Let us now consider a few principles of Montessori education:

- Education must help the child develop its personality in accordance with its nature and possibilities, and at its own rate, so that later it can fulfill its task as an independent, balanced human being in the adult community. The aim, therefore, is always the formation of the total personality, not of independent functions or processes.
- Optimal relationships between children and adults and an optimal environment stimulate and give positive support to this spontaneous inner development. When it occurs, a change takes place in the child called normalization.
- Children want to become adults and, prompted by their inner needs, strive to achieve this goal independently. Education must assist them in this task of inner development. In order to offer them adequate help, it is necessary to understand their psychic activity from the point of view of this final aim.
- Many activities of small children appear meaningless. However, the concentration with which they devote themselves to these activities makes it evident that they are important to them. When children are engaged in such activities, the Montessori teacher must withdraw and allow them to proceed without interruption. Much of the Montessori developmental material has been been constructed to further this kind of indirect preparation for functions that will only later become manifest.
- Only when this happens can the meaning of a single phenomenon be grasped or interpreted in its correct context. Therefore, in Montessori education the self-directed activity of the child is respected. Any attempts to penetrate into the secret of childhood are made through its spontaneous manifestations. Montessori teachers are trained to observe the child and to report on their observations. In this way, the behavior of the child can be studied

in the meaningful context of the whole personality acting in the pedagogical situation.

- The school must be a cultural environment, so that children have the opportunity to become familiar with the basic aspects of their own culture. During the first years of life the child's absorbent mind enables it to incorporate the fundamental patterns of culture it has come in contact with through association with adults. It then proceeds to give them form and content in a personal way. Schools must offer children this possibility for a cultural environment and enlarge their cultural horizon in such a way that not only intellectual, but also spiritual development occurs. The spiritual core of man is already present in children. It directs their psychic development from within by means of special sensitivities and needs that, if given the opportunity, spur the conscious ego of the child to specific activities.

- The Montessori material is constructed to appeal to these inner needs. In addition, it offers children the opportunity to work independently and to have their own experiences with it. Since handling it demands the coordination of different functions, the entire personality is involved. However, one single property is accentuated in each subdivision of the material. A child is thus invited to direct its attention to a special objective quality. The latter is so chosen that it is attuned to a specific psychic activity and requires, at the same time, specific actions for the manipulation of the material. The material itself makes the child aware when something has not been done correctly. Its intelligence is then challenged to find a better solution. In this way the ego functions are differentiated, trained, and integrated without strain, more or less playfully, while the child is stimulated to perform meaningful acts.

- This is possible because the material takes into account the inner needs of the child in the course of its development. It therefore has an inviting character and an emotional appeal. It arouses the interest of the child and stimulates it to activity as well as to concentration. The motto of Montessori education, derived from the utterance of a toddler ("Help me to do it myself"), implies an acknowledgment of the child as a striving being with its own aims and needs. The latter are also indicated by what we call sensitive periods.

- Social development, dealt with in Chapter 2, is one of the fundamental characteristics of Montessori education.
- As far as teaching was concerned, Montessori believed that the emphasis on the intellectual aspect of learning was largely wrong. The role of the personality as a psychosomatic unity in the learning process must be fully acknowledged. No passive absorption, but intelligent action is required. Learning is a dynamic process in which the whole personality of the child must be actively engaged. The Montessori material invites this. The coordination of movements, the self-activity, and the freedom of movement in the classroom characteristic of Montessori education are also applications of this principle.
- In conclusion, it may be mentioned that a free choice of activity, which confronts the child with alternatives and which therefore teaches it to become independent, is a Montessori principle par excellence. The formal, classical approach to education excludes, by definition, the possibility of taking this fundamental aspect of man's existence into account. Imposing the same task on an entire group degrades an alternative to a necessity.

It is clear from this brief statement of the principles followed in applying the Montessori method that they are consistent with the principles of modern psychology. Let us now examine the scientific method employed in Montessori schools to see how it relates to other methods employed in modern psychology. Method is the most important characteristic of all science. The only difference between an unscientific opinion and a scientific judgment is that the latter is based on method. Having a method is essentially no more than working in a systematic way. It is a kind of discipline, or self-control, that consists of constantly querying whether and how far that which one asserts is really based on experience or supported by it. Experimentation is no doubt the most ideal method of investigation in the empirical sciences. Its advantages are not exceeded by those of any other method. Laboratory experimentation, however, has practical limitations. That is why ways are sought to retain the advantages of the experimental method in the systematic study of phenomena which cannot be studied in the laboratory. One of the most important ways of doing this is through field experiments, where the field is a normal environment, for example, a school. Even closer to everyday experience is so-called action-research in which a community (such as a school) cooperates with experts in the research program. These experts not only investigate existing conditions, but seek to improve them. Such research therefore has a normative character. Another method of investigation outside of the laboratory is to make the observer or researcher a member of the group under observation. The use of this method in psychoanalysis and in Montessori education was discussed in Chapter 1. However, making and recording observations, it should be remembered, is a very difficult task for most people. If teachers are required to do this, it is important to give considerable attention to such matters in their training. Otherwise, the danger of mechanization and rigidity will be great. It is precisely because a scientific attitude requiring constant observation is important that the Montessori method makes great demands on teachers wishing to apply it. All the scientific methods described above are compatible with Montessori education, although there will be differences in the way they are applied in practice.

If we view the relationship between Montessori education and modern psychology as a whole, the following can be observed: Until World War II, applied psychology was predominantly laboratory psychology. Montessori education, which is based on an empirical experiment with children in concrete life situations, could do very little with it. As I have mentioned, Maria Montessori herself was so struck by and involved in what she called the discovery of the child that she never felt the need to build up a theoretical system. It was not theories that were important to her, but the child itself. The revelations of its spontaneous behavior touched her so profoundly that she devoted the rest of her life to acting on its behalf. Indeed she referred to herself as an "ambassadress for the cause of the child."

Since World War II psychology has developed rapidly, and there has been a growing interest in the concrete behavior of man in ordinary, everyday situations. Because of this, the divergence between Montessori education and psychology has decreased, and a possibility of bridging the gap between them may well exist. I hope that the thoughts presented here will be a spur to efforts in this direction.

NOTES

1. From a report in the daily paper *De Dordtenaar* (August 12, 1950), p. 5. Requests for more details of this case from UNESCO and Vellard have remained unanswered.

2. See Theodora Kroeber, *ISHI in Two Worlds* (Berkeley and Los Angeles: University of California Press, 1962).

4/ THE PSYCHOLOGICAL VALUE OF WORK IN SCHOOL

An endeavor to assess the psychological value of work in school necessitates a summary of both the psychological significance of Maria Montessori's contribution to human knowledge and work as a human phenomenon. These two main issues must in turn be related to the educational situation. It will then be possible to evaluate work within the school setting and, at the same time, to estimate the psychological merits of the Montessori approach and traditional education as it is practiced today.

The driving force giving impetus and direction to Montessori's thinking was a truly profound vision of man and his position in the world. This vision was based on her conviction that when man appeared in the world a new species came into being. She called for a new beginning in the study of child development based on this conviction. It was her anthropological orientation that eventually resulted in her "discovery" of the child. This discovery consisted of a realization of the specific function of the child in the formation of man and as the link between generations in mankind's cultural evolutions. The behavior patterns typical of the human species are not hereditary—only the abilities to form them are. Man reaches maturity only in his postnatal state, when he is already exposed to environmental influences. The continuation of the embryonic process that occurs after birth is of a psychological order because it requires the active participation of the individual involved. The child has special powers that facilitate self-construction: an absorbent mind and sensitive periods. But it needs the help of adults. Education has a fundamental role in the formation of man, and its foremost aim should be to offer adequate aid and stimulation to the intricate process of inner construction.

Of course, we all realize that whatever we are now, whatever we can do, is the result of a previous period of development, and a process of learning influenced by the education we have received. Montessori, however, believed that a lack of education would not merely restrict our capabilities as adults but would, if extreme enough, preclude the possibility of even becoming human beings. Let us, for example, imagine a healthy normal baby separated from its mother at birth and brought up with the best of foods in an air-conditioned, soundproof space with sufficient light and all other material conditions mechanically regulated in an optimal way but empty of further objects and human contacts. If such a being remained alive through puberty, which in itself would be extremely unlikely, it would not be a human being but merely a creature resembling a human being. It would not be a question of its simply having lost fifteen years of tutoring that it would have to make up. It would actually possess none of the attributes we consider essentially human and of which we are so proud. If such a luckless creature were admitted to society at maturity, it would not be able to recover the ground it had lost. It would remain a misfit, however long it might be kept alive, in spite of being given whatever it had been deprived of during its isolation. It would, of course, be too cruel to prove this by an experiment. Humanity is often cruel, however, and there have been instances where children who were deprived in one way or another lost forever certain faculties inherent in human beings. A well-known historical example is Dr. Jean Itard's account of the *"sauvage de l' Aveyron,"* a wolf child found in the woods shortly after the French Revolution. The description of Dr. Itard's experiences with this child interested and inspired Montessori long before she started her pedagogical work.

Let us now consider work as a human phenomenon. In one of his relatively rare discussions of work, Freud remarks, "After primal man had discovered that it lay in his own hands, literally, to improve his lot on earth by working, it cannot have been a matter of indifference to him whether another man worked with him or against him. The other man acquired the value for him of a fellow worker, with whom it was useful to live together."[1] I should like to add "and to achieve peaceful coexistence and collaboration he invented a language to communicate with him." In the quotation above, which one could easily believe to have come from Montessori's writings, Freud defines the essence of work as a human phenomenon. What he actually tells us is that man has a purpose in life. This purpose is to improve his lot, which necessitates an intrinsic relation between him and his environment. It also brings him to discover that it is only through his own activity, namely by using his intelligence and its tools, the hands, that he can change his environment. Work is a fundamental feature of the human being as a species, and an adaptive, creative, and social function par excellence. Although its meaning, social role, and specific objectives have changed throughout the centuries and have differed from one community to another, it has always maintained its position as one of the main spheres of human behavior.

It is curious that relatively little has been written about work as a human phenomenon. Even in modern studies on the subject, the ability to work, which may well be called a major human phenomenon, has received little attention. It has evidently been taken for granted. Psychologists have given much attention to the problem of work, and there is a vast literature on the subject, but most of it concerns secondary aspects of the problem. It does not answer the question of why people work at all, or why they fail to do so. Learning theory, which pretends to give an answer, does so only in terms of conditioning. In reality, this is only one aspect of a very complex phenomenon. It is also the less human one, for it deals with that which man has in common, on the one hand, with animals and, on the other, with machines. Its failure to explain adequately some of the crucial phenomena in humans has finally engendered a promising reaction in the direction of a rehumanization of psychology.

The contribution of Professor Walter S. Neff of New York University to an understanding of work and human behavior is of special interest.[2] His comprehensive approach coincides in principle with that of Montessori. As a clinical psychologist, he has worked closely for a number of years with people for whom work is a major difficulty. Drawing on this experience, he has undertaken to study work as a human phenomenon from all relevant angles. He has focused on the ability to work in its own right and also in relation to the general problems of the human personality. He sees it, therefore, in its true complexity. His definition of work coincides with the views expressed above in connection with Freud's remarks. The latter, however, are in regard to work by adults, not the ability to work as such, nor how it develops. Neff endeavors to investigate this process. He sees the ability to work as an aspect of the development of the personality, with which it is interrelated, although it is eventually differentiated into a relatively autonomous sphere of behavior. He does not see it as limited to particular aptitudes and skills, but as adaptive and hence transactional. He thereby acknowledges the different stages of development.

Neff suggests that the conditions for becoming a worker "may be certain necessary kinds of experiences in early and middle childhood." This is interesting in connection with Montessori's sensitive periods. (American psychologists refer to "critical periods.") However, Neff's insight is not sufficient for him to overcome certain ingrained prejudices. It works to some extent with regard to emotional influences, but there it stops.

In summarizing the components of what he calls the work personality, Neff states three conclusions: First, the general source of the will to work is the precepts of society. The fact that society expects an individual to play a productive role determines his behavior, not inner promptings at various stages of development. Second, the critical periods for the formation of the work personality are middle childhood and adolescence. Third, the compulsion to work is initially entirely external to the organism, but it becomes internalized to varying degrees and in different forms.

In enunciating these conclusions, Professor Neff totally abandons his original goal, which was to study the meaning of work in general and to focus on the ability to work in light of the developmental process. In making the three points above, he has in mind a special form of work: that of the adult. He has evidently looked for the earliest period in childhood when such work occurs, which is, of course, when the child goes to school for formal instruction at approximately six years of age. Thus he sees this as the first of the critical periods relevant to work. However, the behavior pattern of children at this stage results from an integration of experiences related to critical periods in previous stages, during which their ability to work was developed to the extent of permitting them to attend school. If the compulsion to work is initially entirely external to the organism, what is the significance of Neff's first critical period? Perhaps by then children have been sufficiently manipulated and indoctrinated by adults, that they conform to the precepts of society without protest! In his introduction, Neff writes, "One of our major concerns will be to consider the manner in which a non-working child becomes a working adult." Apparently, this transformation is to be achieved by molding it from the outside. We are back to the age-old prejudice of adults who think that because a child functions in a different way it is void of the qualities one encounters in adults. In actual fact, the child is building these qualities within itself, but in its own way.

The concept of development is inconceivable without a goal. There must be something in a developing being to guide the process from within. Everything that manifests itself as new in that long-range process must be the result of a period of indirect preparation. If that preparation process is a type of adaptation, which must not be confused with either adjustment or conformism, then there must be something that drives the child to shape its own behavior patterns to harmonize with its environment. Otherwise it would be like a circus animal being drilled to perform in a way that was alien to it. Behaviorists may believe that this is the case, but I do not. This kind of view, which is dominant in traditional education, precludes the development of the kind of flexible work behavior that is needed in the world today.

Before psychoanalysis, it was believed that because the sexual function in the adult form had its onset at puberty, infant sexuality did not exist. Neff has adopted the same attitude in regard to work. In reality its roots must be looked for in the very first crucial formative period of the spiritual embryo. Some time ago, I was at a wedding reception. The bridegroom's sister was helping to receive guests, so she let her husband babysit with their one-and-a-half-year-old boy. The father took up a position with his back to one of those stray tables where the food offered remains nearly untouched. As his little boy was at the age when humans grab and examine whatever they can lay their hands on, his father kept him on his arm so that he could not reach the objects on the table. From time to time, the father gave the boy a cookie, but instead of eating it himself, the child enjoyed pushing it in his father's mouth. As I do not much like receptions and am always fascinated by the spontaneous reactions of young children, I parked myself behind the father's back, facing the child and holding a pretzel stick in my mouth like a cigarette. I wanted to see whether the child would do the same thing with me as he had with his father. He looked, with an intent, inquiring expression, first at my eyes, then at the stick in my mouth, then again at my eyes. He hesitated as if he were considering whether I was a friend or foe. Finally, the temptation became irresistible. Very carefully, he stuck out his right index finger and, with the precision of a scientist working in a laboratory, he slowly brought his arm forward until the tip of his outstretched finger contacted the end of the pretzel and gently pushed the stick inside my mouth. His eyes watched me carefully to see when the pretzel completely disappeared. When it was gone, I took a new one and the child began the whole performance again, but now without any hesitancy, fully engrossed in what it was doing. When there were not too many sticks left, I let the same one reappear. The child continued to repeat his pushing action with enormous concentration until all of a sudden, he grabbed the stick out of my mouth and ate it with a beaming face. The cycle of activity was completed. From a hygienic point of view, it was most deplorable, of course, but as a manifestation of a human being in the act of building within himself the ability to work, it was too precious to stop.

What a perfect coordination of intelligence, perception, and movement, and what an intensity of absorption was demonstrated in what to Neff would have been a senseless little game. True, the activity had no apparent purpose; it was performed for its own sake, and it was thus play according to his definitions of work and play. But it did have an unconscious purpose. It was not directed toward mastering the outer environment, but toward the construction of what Montessori called "the organs of the mind." These mental organs are formed by this kind of interaction between the inner and outer world, the motivation for which comes from within. This motivation manifests itself through the sensitive periods. However, even after their conclusion, the urge to learn, to form one's own personality, adapted to both one's individual potentialities and the conditions of one's environment (and hence the ability to work), accompanies the growing individual throughout the whole lengthy period of youth. Specific sensitive periods end when they have performed their function or when the maturational limits within which they can occur have been passed, but the intensive attraction to the environment, the love for it, remains a basic attitude of the growing individual. At least, it does if it is not inhibited or repressed by inner anxieties or by restrictive measures or taboos imposed by adults.

Education should take this into consideration and use it as a guide in structuring the pedagogical situation. We have discussed the fact that the task of educators is to help growing human beings to develop. They can do so by offering children an environment that stimulates their inner potentialities at different stages of development. The psychological value of work in school depends on whether we succeed in doing this when we decide how to organize a school: what to include in the curriculum and which method of instruction we should follow. The children themselves should serve as our guide. Our success is determined by their responses. If they work with concentration and pleasure, then we have found the link with that inner force which directs their development. If their spirit (a forbidden word in psychology!) is not touched, they may comply with our demands for work; but the psychological value of their work will be restricted to a more or less mechanical learning of techniques. This process does not involve the total personality, and consequently has little formative value.

To illustrate this point, I sometimes use the case of a male patient, twenty-eight years old, who came to me for psychoanalytic treatment. He complained of anxiety, crying bouts, depression, and an inability to work. He had not worked since leaving secondary school. His first breakdown took place at college. It was followed by similar crises every time he tried a new occupation. At last he gave up all attempts at working and began living a solitary, inactive life in an attic. He had lost his father, whom he was very fond of, when he was three years old. This death was followed by a sequence of traumatic events, including a move to a different country and a change in the family's social status that disrupted his rather paradisical world drastically. He tried to save himself from this emotional wreckage by warding off reality, taking refuge in a fantasy world. His attitude toward the outer world was one of passive conformism, which actually covered up deep feelings of rancor and superiority.

At the age of four, he was sent to a Montessori infant school, where he felt completely at a loss. The freedom especially terrified him. By allowing him independence and holding him responsible for his own actions, the school challenged him to leave the security of his self-made prison. His mode of existence was jeopardized, and he felt paralyzed. He was then moved to a Dalton school where he was given specific tasks and told more or less how long he was supposed to work at them. The rest of the time he could work by himself, unless he wished to ask something. He managed to avoid doing that as he was intelligent and did not need assistance. He did not mix with the other pupils, but he appeared happy to be left in peace. He proved to be a brilliant pupil throughout both elementary and high school, and his high marks indicated that he would have an easy time at college. Instead, he collapsed there.

Of course, he had always remained difficult at home, leading a solitary life in his room. He considered his schoolwork a tedious duty which he had to perform in order to keep exigent adults off his back and be free to withdraw into an imaginary world where he found solace for his wounded ego in fantasies of grandeur. However, as long as his work at school was satisfactory, things went reasonably well. He passed for a normal boy, although he was not. It took seven years of analysis to restore his grip on reality and enable him to find a meaning in life again.

The case of this patient was not very unusual. A number of students sent to me by their university health care department for counseling had very similar histories. They had achieved apparent social adjustment by complying dutifully with the requirements of the school's curriculum, without, however, taking part in school life proper, and they had deep-seated emotional problems that went unnoticed. What is the psychological value of work in school in these cases? Clearly, it is as a defense. Normal development has stagnated at some stage, partly inhibiting the process of adaptation. This neurosis, however, has not affected the ability to work, because of the relative autonomy of this sphere of behavior. The work demanded by schools is one-sided, focused only on certain aspects of intellectual functioning. Society puts so much value on success in this quarter that it permits these individuals, through conformity, to build up a fake state of normality. However, when they leave the protected and artificial environment of the school, they collapse, like hothouse plants exposed for the first time to the hardships of a natural climate.

It is interesting to note in this connection that the psychological importance of education for the formation of man in the different stages of development, whether at school or elsewhere, is in reverse proportion to the value usually accorded it by society. This is reflected clearly in the progressive level of training, social status, and remuneration of the educators involved: the domestic personnel caring for infants at home, the workers in child-care centers, the teachers in preprimary, elementary, and secondary schools, and finally, university professors at the top of the academic tree. Thanks to the ever-growing specialization and mechanization of instruction, the latter really contribute very little to the formation of the student's personality, and their role in this connection is on the decline.

Let us now consider how the educational process resulting from the Montessori approach coincides with pedagogical psychology. In a historical survey of the development of pedagogical psychology, Professor Max Hillebrand stresses the necessity of an anthropological orientation in both pedagogy and psychology for a fundamental understanding of the human being. This is an acknowledgment of the basic thesis that "man as *animal educandum* is a being that without learning and education cannot become man."[3] He points out that education cannot work without the concept of dispositions (Montessori's potentialities). It aims at them as its result and effect. Educators must find ways to reach the deeper layers of the personality, permitting the dispositions to come into play. Professor

Heinrich Roth, in concluding a discussion on problems of educability, remarks that education must of necessity appeal to the child's growing self-insight and auto-education. What is most important is the reinforcement of the child's increasing ability to act independently in a responsible way.[4]

This may suffice to show that the Montessori approach to work in the school corresponds to what is considered basic when education is oriented toward the formation of man. Traditional education in a classical setting, on the other hand, concerns itself too exclusively with the transfer of knowledge, ignoring its responsibility with regard to the inner development of personality.

Montessori considered the ability to work to be an important aspect of the independence of the individual throughout life. As early as adolescence she believed that economic independence based on one's own initiative was essential to a sense of well-being. Succeeding by one's own efforts, she felt, and at the same time being in contact with the reality of life that work represents, enhances the personality. This is true all through adult life and into old age. It is not the kind of work one devotes oneself to that is of most importance, but the principle of work itself. "All work is noble," she wrote. "The only ignoble thing is to live without working." Intellectual work and manual work are complementary and "equally essential in a civilized existence."[5]

A society constructed without an awareness of man's need for work would be a hazardous one indeed for man's future health. However, it is not likely that such a society will ever be built. It is only the work that can be done by machines that man may be relieved of. He will still have the ability to work, and the inner urge to do so, if it is not nipped in the bud when he is a child.

Montessori gave a new orientation to work in school because she realized its psychological value. Hopefully, a sufficient number of educators will share this insight, and the responsibility that goes with it, so that there will be real and lasting changes in the educational approach of the future.

NOTES

1. Sigmund Freud, *Civilization and Its Discontents*, standard ed., vol. 21 (London: Hogarth Press, 1953), p. 99.

2. See Walter S. Neff, *Work and Human Behavior* (New York: Atherton Press, 1968).

3. Max Josef Hillebrand, "Begriffsbestimmung und Geschichtliche Entwicklung der Pädagogischen Psychologie," *Handbuch der Psychologie*, vol. 10 (Göttingen, 1959), p. 46.

4. Heinrich Roth, "Problem der Bildsamkeit und Erziehungsfähigkeit in der Psychologischen Forschung," ibid., p. 90.

5. Maria Montessori, *From Childhood to Adolescence* (New York: Schocken Books, 1973), p. 103.

5 / MONTESSORI AND THE PROCESS OF EDUCATION

We shall now consider the process of education within the special setting of the school. It should be clear from previous chapters that school is only one aspect of the educational process in Montessori's thinking. The Montessori approach is based on the revolutionary idea that education has an indispensable role in the formation of man. Without some kind of interaction with a human being whereby a minimum of cultural data is transmitted, a newborn child cannot complete the basic development necessary to become one of its species. This conception determines the aim and the general principles of Montessori education.

This aim is to offer adequate aid to the development of the growing human being. Education starts at birth, and therefore concerns parents as well as all other adults who take care of a child in the different milieus in which it grows. It should be directed toward the future and we should take into account the whole continuum of growth in establishing its objective. Also, to be scientific, education must be based on a theory of development.

This last point, which may seem self-evident, is in fact little understood by educators even today, and is far from being applied in any comprehensive way. The only American-made plan to do this that I have come across is one by Professor Helena Miller of Duquesne University.[1] I find it promising because it is not an outcome of simple theorizing. Rather, it has grown out of twenty-seven years of experience teaching "students of every age level, from all strata of society, in every type of school."

The technique used to educate children must be one of love. I do not use the word in the sentimental sense, of course, but to designate that most powerful of all emotions by which human beings are attracted to and relate to persons and objects that gratify their most fundamental needs. The psychoanalytic approach to education is based on a similar principle and reaches similar conclusions. For example:

Good education follows the development of the child.
The emotional relationship with the educator is the central aspect of all education. Everything that benefits it, benefits education.
The child's capacity to tolerate tensions can only be increased if tensions never surpass what the child can stand.

Progress from one phase of development to the next is optimal when there has been sufficient gratification: not too much, not too little.
A good educator should have a positive attitude towards the instinctual life of the child, and understand its developmental potential.
The good educator offers the child material adapted to his development and at the moment in time when he is most ready to respond.
Secrets should be avoided in education.[2]

The object of education is an entity in the process of becoming a human being. Education should not focus on special functions, faculties, or skills, but on the whole personality. Educational planning must be longitudinal, taking into account the continuity as well as the discontinuity of different maturational sequences. Adults must stimulate and guide the spontaneous activity of children by offering them an environment that appeals to their urge for self-realization, and by discouraging behavior that may block it. Respect for a child's personality and trust in its inner potentialities are prerequisites to the establishment of an adequate educational alliance.

The dynamic aspect of education stems from a recognition of the child's relation to the world. Its open communication with the world is a fundamental factor in its development. This gives the concept of adaptation a central position in the process of education. There is a two-way dynamism involving exploration of and adaptation to the outer world on the one hand, and insight into an organization of the inner world on the other. These two aspects of education are interlinked, and result from the spontaneous activity of the child in its environment. Adults are the representatives of the outer world and the most important source of information and guidance for the child. Older children also play an important role in this connection.

The situational aspect of education involves the prepared environment. Man is not born with preestablished behavior patterns but with the ability to form them during youth. He does this through his personal experiences in his interaction with the environment. These experiences are internalized, and thus structure his inner world.

The ego functions, including intelligence, are developed in this way. Intellectual growth "depends upon internalizing events into a 'storage system' that corresponds to the environment. It is this system that makes possible the child's increasing ability to go beyond the information encountered on a single occasion. He does this by making predictions and extrapolations from his stored model of the world." [3] Montessori's term for this "storage system" is the absorbent mind.

This is a very important issue, often disregarded or misunderstood. It is of the utmost relevance in deciding what type of assistance is the most adequate in connection with intellectual growth. It is a common misconception that children, being so inexperienced and incapable of dealing with abstractions, should be offered an introduction to the world in sections chosen by an adult and made to size, starting with pieces of their immediate environment and progressing in ever-expanding circles to more distant and complex situations.

If this kind of approach is followed, young adults, who are supposed to be ready to start functioning independently in the world, will have a very restricted, haphazard, and arbitrary knowledge of it at their disposal. Unfortunately, this is often the case.

However, this presumed model of education does not correspond with the actual way in which children can be observed to acquire knowledge. Young children learn a mass of things without any particular form of teaching. By the age of three or four, they have already formed the basic patterns of their personality. They are therefore prepared to take a major step toward further independence by entering a new milieu, that of school. Nobody has, up to this point, separated and reduced sections of the world for them to digest. They have been confronted from an early age with the world at large and their "storage systems" are well stocked. What they internalize at any given time is never entirely new. There has been a previous internal and indirect preparation for it.

The choice of what is internalized and the different activities involved are determined by a child from within. Nobody would know how to teach it language, for example. How could anyone show it how to select, out of all the sounds in its environment, those of language, or how to exercise the organs of speech and reproduce sounds in order to express itself. The child does this, and indeed much more, on its own. This is why it must be offered what is necessary or useful for it and then left free to function independently. Maria Montessori originally used the term "auto-education" to designate this process.

Many aspects of personality can be tested, and some predictions can be made; but no one can predict what the destiny of any one individual will be. The only thing we can do is offer every child the opportunity to develop according to its own potentialities, and to acquire new perspectives that will facilitate its exploration and internalization of the cultural world around it. This is the purpose of the prepared environment, including the Montessori materials.

Any application of Montessori education derives its meaning from these general principles. To see how it can contribute to the mainstream of innovation with respect to educational process in the school setting, I have chosen relevant sections of Jerome Bruner's brilliant report on the Woods Hole conference as focal points for discussion.

This conference, which was held on Cape Cod in 1959, was called by the National Academy of Science. Some thirty-five renowned scientists, scholars, and educators participated in the discussions on the problems of modern education. Bruner, who was chairman of the conference, published his report under the title *The Process of Education*.[4] I shall not follow the same sequence of topics in comparing my views with those described by Bruner, but the headings are the same, and indicate the portion of the book to which they refer.

Readiness for Learning

Under this heading the hypothesis is presented that any subject can be taught effectively in some intellectually honest form to any child at any stage of development. It is called a bold hypothesis, although no evidence exists, it is stated, to contradict it, and much has been amassed that supports it. It was certainly a bold hypothesis when Montessori started to test it in 1907, and the world was startled by the results she obtained. Since then, her original experiment has been repeated and elaborated upon in schools the world over. When the right methods are used, one still sees the same results. Her thesis, therefore, should not really be called a hypothesis any more, bold or otherwise. However, it is certainly a hopeful sign that scientists have started to take it seriously at last.

If one asks oneself why it has taken so long for this to happen, the only possible answer is that there is evidently a prejudice in the realm of pedagogy and developmental psychology with regard to the young child. This has so far prevented any widespread scientific consideration of what can be observed with convincing clarity in Montessori schools.

The existence of a biased attitude within this realm of science was confirmed by J. McVicker Hunt in a treatise called "The Psychological Basis for Using Pre-School Enrichment as an Antidote for Cultural Deprivation."[5] In it, he outlined six "beliefs" dominating the thinking of psychological theoreticians until the mid-1960s that led to biased conclusions. One of these beliefs was that preschool children have not reached the level of maturation necessary to understand certain fundamental ideas required for a specific type of operational thinking. Any attempt to stimulate such operational thinking was regarded as overburdening the child intellectually, generating frustrations that would inhibit intellectual performance later. Progressive education consequently overemphasized the importance of freedom, fantasy, "creativity," and self-expression.

These are of vital importance to the child, but they must be integrated into a comprehensive setting where other aspects of the personality, particularly intellectual growth, are also taken into account. If this growth is ignored, children's fundamental needs are neglected. Psychoanalytic experience shows that this tends to foster aggressive behavior. Frustrations are simply displaced from one realm of psychic functioning to another, from the emotional to the cognitive sphere.

It is not clear to me why it is so difficult to accept that if maturation is sufficient to permit what Piaget calls "concrete operations" it can only be thanks to an inner development that has been going on in the preceding period. It is particularly puzzling if one knows that the child has developed a quantity of functions pertinent to intelligence in that period. Nothing comes out of the blue in a developmental process. In addition, what is acquired in the first six years of life in terms of learning becomes a characteristic, forming part and parcel of the personality set-up, as both Montessori education and psychoanalysis have demonstrated.

Although Bruner does not preclude the possibility of instructing younger children, he seems inclined to share the position of the Geneva school, which does not endeavor to do so because their investigation has shown that the "preoperational" child (i. e., the preschool child) lacks the concept of reversibility.[6] As this concept is basic to understanding fundamental ideas underlying mathematics and physics, it would be useless to try introducing these subjects at that stage. Bruner remarks that teachers are in general severely limited in transmitting concepts to a "preoperational" child, even in a highly intuitive manner.

Both statements may be true, but I have some objections to make. The Geneva school rightly describes the mental development of the preschool child as being resultant of the child's manipulating the world through action. My point is that this manipulation is evidently necessary to obtain the experience from which the first conceptual thinking eventually emerges. It does not happen without previous indirect preparation.

This is one of the fundamental discoveries of Maria Montessori. It is to her credit that she devised a means of introducing highly abstract concepts in a concrete way so that children could explore them at this early stage. This means is the already mentioned "materialized abstractions," materials that isolate a general principle or concept. A child manipulates them, performing actions (which it loves), and in the meantime, through this sensomotoric experience, gets acquainted with the principle or concept involved. It is also taught the terms that go with it. This experience quickens its progress toward the next stage, that of "operational thinking." [7]

The Geneva School

It is particularly bewildering to me that the later developments in Montessori education have been ignored by the Geneva school. Jean Piaget, the grand old man of this school, knew Maria Montessori very well and was, in fact, president of the Swiss Montessori Society in the 1930s. He worked along very much the same lines as Montessori, basing his thinking on direct observation of the behavior of children, and taking into account the sequences of development he observed and the interaction with the environment (albeit emphasizing in my opinion a bit too much the role of the latter).

I believe this overemphasis is related to the two things I find fault with in his otherwise very impressive contribution. First, Piaget seems to identify what is outwardly observable in the child's behavior or what it verbalizes, with that which takes place in its inner world. This is a mistake made by many other behavioral scientists, and is, in my opinion, the result of an unfortunate prejudice.

To give a simple example, most adults have not cultivated their artistic potential to the extent that they are able to draw an accurate and realistic picture of another person whom they know very well. Nonetheless, I am quite certain that they have such a picture in their own minds. There is clearly, then, a gap between what is in the mind and what can be expressed. This is particularly true in learning processes, when one is dealing with something previously unknown. First, there is a passive acquisition of the new information. This is assimilated, but it is not yet internalized. Only when data becomes part of a person is he able to actively use it.

In the case of development, the process is even longer. Here, there is first an unconscious acquisition of information which corresponds to a particular function that is to be formed at a given stage of maturation. We can, therefore, be certain that a child's first primitive drawings of people are not the same as the image of human beings in its mind. (I have in mind the well-known drawing of a kind of egg with four sticks sticking out of it designating arms and legs, each with five stripes for fingers and toes, and a smaller egg for the face, with rudimentary signs to indicate the eyes, nose, mouth, and hairs.)

What has happened is that the child has perceived a great quantity of people. It has elaborated its impressions of them to the extent that it can reduce them to a scheme common to all, which reflects their essence, as it were. This rudimentary drawing is the result of an abstraction. It has taken place unconsciously, that is true, but it has nevertheless taken place. The product cannot be used to judge the capacity of the child's mind for abstraction. Something can be learned from it about the way in which this inner activity is manifested in observable behavior, but this is not the same thing. The child's capacity for sensory discrimination, the quality of its perception of reality, its sense of proportions, its artistic evaluation of pictoral representations in general, cannot be determined from what it has drawn. Yet this is what Piaget tends to do with the material he assembles from his observations.

My second objection to Piaget is that he then proceeds to interpret and categorize this material using standards of adult logic.[8] The system is perfect, but the image of the child that results from it is distorted. In one of her writings [9] Montessori discusses the results of judging the newborn child morphologically by adult standards. From this standpoint, it is a monster. She also pointed out how painters in the Middle Ages and later, not yet being conscious of the morphological differences between adults and children, gave children the proportions of adults, so that they resembled dwarfs. These painters were very skilled in perceiving and reproducing reality. However, their prejudice regarding what children were like prevented them from representing children as they really were.

I believe that something similar occurs in Piaget's psychology, and that it is the reason he overlooked the fundamental discovery of Montessori mentioned above. I have discussed this matter at length because I am convinced that no real progress can be made in the study of intellectual growth if this a priori attitude prevails. The view of the child as an imperfect adult is based on prejudice, and only if this prejudice is rooted out can unbiased research on human development be done. It is particularly important that this be done now that scientists of Bruner's stature have, at last, paved the way for an approach to education based on this kind of research.

We can already predict, from Montessori's experience, some of the phenomena that unprejudiced researchers will encounter with regard to the readiness for learning of the preschool child in a prepared environment. For example, children have an inner need to learn. If they receive adequate help, they respond to this need with an astounding intensity of involvement and concentration on a given task, and, what is more, they perform the task fully. They derive satisfaction from their own activity, which is highly meaningful to them, not from the teacher's appreciation of their work or grades. The acquisition of information is felt to be a discovery. The formation of a new function is experienced as a conquest. The children's egos are strengthened, and they develop a love of work and a respect for the environment that offers them the sources of the satisfaction described above.

This is, in my opinion, of particular importance in our time. If human dignity and joy in living are not to be smothered by the Industrial Age, the true value of work as an aspect of man's creativity and cosmic task must be restored. This is only possible if education takes into consideration the earliest roots of work, the activities related to the inner construction of the personality, and not merely directed toward an external goal. It is from this source that the child gets its motivation to learn, and it is a strong one. Teaching has a developmental function only if it corresponds to this motivation.

The child's own response is the best guide in this respect. If it is one of interest and concentration, then one is on the right track. I am, of course, speaking of children who have gone through the process of normalization. On this foundation a curriculum can indeed be built around the great issues, principles, and values that a society deems worthy of the continual concern of its members. This can be accomplished even on the preprimary level, as Montessori education has demonstrated with a great deal of success.

The Importance of Structure

In discussing the function of learning to serve the future, Bruner points to the distinction made by psychologists between learning as a transfer of specific training (the utility of which is limited in the main to skills) and learning as a transfer of principles and attitudes that involves the continual broadening and deepening of knowledge in terms of basic and general ideas. He rightly states that this second type of transfer is at the heart of the educational process. He also states that a great deal of research is needed to know what it takes to produce this kind of learning but that "it would seem that an important ingredient is a sense of excitement about discovery—of regularities, of previously unrecognized relations and similarities between ideas, [and the] resulting sense of self-confidence in one's abilities."[10] I believe that Montessori education can serve as a focal point for much of this research.

I have already explained the function of the Montessori material. However, I wish here to connect it with the concept of a transfer of principles and attitudes just mentioned. This is an area even Montessori-trained teachers sometimes find difficult to understand. The role of the Montessori material is not to present all knowledge in concrete form. That would be too difficult for a child to understand from verbal instructions only. Nor is it to break down a complex thing into its elements. If that were the case, it would only serve the more limited goal of learning in the sense of a specific transfer of training.

Teachers who think of the Montessori material in this way still have in mind the old conception of school education. Consequently, they find the Montessori material too limited and proceed to "improve" matters by flooding the classroom with quantities of additional material. I can testify from my own experience to what extremes of monklike devotion and patience these misguided Montessori teachers can go. What time and money they are willing to spend to produce this mass of most attractive-looking ballast! And how proud they are of it.

It places one in a most uncomfortable position. It is hard to react adequately when a loyal puppy jumps into our sitting room to deposit a dead sparrow it has gone to great lengths to catch for us. It looks at us with tail wagging, full of expectation, waiting for its reward. Still, a dead sparrow is what it has brought us. Psychologically speaking, what these teachers actually do is destroy the true function of the Montessori material.

The material is intended to facilitate a transfer of nonspecific knowledge, that of a general idea or principle that can later be used as a basis for recognizing special cases or applications of it. Montessori material should be developmental. It should be limited to essentials, and should be constructed so that a particular general idea or principle is isolated. The children then become conscious of this idea or principle by handling the material in the way they are instructed. The built-in controls of error show them when they are wrong. The insight they gain into the underlying general principle or idea is felt as a personal discovery. They are fascinated by it and will repeat an exercise time and again with great concentration until they have fully absorbed the principle or concept it illustrates.

The subsequent applications of what is learned in this way may be limitless. And, as Bruner writes, "The best way to create interest in a subject is to render it worth knowing, which means to make the knowledge gained usable in one's thinking beyond the situation in which the learning has occurred." [11] Educational material should facilitate this kind of learning. Classrooms should not be cluttered with other material that distracts the child. For example, if smelling bottles were specifically for the development of smelling as a skill, one might well want to have dozens and dozens of different fragrances all bottled and ready for matching. Our young students would soon be connoisseurs of odors. However, the purpose of smelling bottles is not a knowledge of odors, but an awakening of the sense of smell, since the intellect is built upon the alertness of the senses. A few bottles suffice for this purpose. A huge quantity would not only be confusing, but would result in overkill.

Intuitive and Analytic Thinking

In stressing the importance of a student's intuitive, rather than formal, understanding of subjects, Bruner advises that we should distinguish between inarticulate genius and articulate idiocy. He maintains that the emphasis of much of traditional schooling and traditional types of examinations leads to the latter. Students can reproduce verbal or numerical formulas, but they have no ability to use them in a meaningful way. Bruner suggests that intuitive thinking should complement analytic thinking, and that curriculums should be planned accordingly. "The objective of education," he points out, "is not the production of self-confident fools." [12]

I fully agree. I should like to stress in this connection that curriculums should not be planned in such a manner that each subject is treated as a separate entity, disconnected from everything else. At a time when ecology was still a fairly unknown branch of science, Montessori proposed to introduce it as a vehicle for the coordination of different subjects and as a model to be adopted in other fields of instruction. In this way, the interrelatedness of natural phenomena would become apparent to the children. Furthermore, thinking would be combined with action and experimentation, so that not only the mind but the whole personality of the child would be involved.

Aids to Teaching

With regard to the use of technical devices other than the Montessori material (such as films, tapes, and television) as aids to teaching, we can, in the main, adhere to Bruner's conclusion that "the teacher's task as communicator, model, and identification figure can be supported by a wise use of a variety of devices that expand experience, clarify it, and give it personal significance." [13] Such devices must, however, fit in with the general approach described at the beginning of this chapter in order to serve their purpose. This cannot be stressed sufficiently.

This means that whatever the teacher brings into the environment must have a definite purpose, and it must have a definite purpose for individual children. The teacher determines this purpose from observing the children. It is wise to remember that a material added to the environment is stimulating to a child. If it has always been there, it becomes part of the scenery and is not noticed. What is not in use should be removed, no matter how professional it makes the environment appear. Classrooms where this principle is not observed sometimes look like they should be captioned "IBM for Children." Another principle to remember is that it is the adult who has a purpose in bringing material into the classroom. The children are not aware of this purpose. This lack of awareness is what leads them to feel that they are in fact teaching themselves. "I just taught myself" is a phrase that is often heard in a good classroom. If the opposite is true, if the children feel it is the material that is doing the teaching, its presence in the environment is suspect.

Motives for Learning

Although this topic has already been discussed, I would like to conclude by quoting once more from Bruner's remarks on the subject, for they indicate what Montessori's contribution to contemporary education can be. "Motives for learning," he writes,

> must be kept from going passive in an age of spectatorship, they must be based as much as possible upon the arousal of interest in what there is to be learned, and they must be kept broad and diverse in expression. The danger signs of meritocracy and a new form of competitiveness are already in evidence. Already it is possible to see where advance planning can help. Such planning, and the research to support it, should be given priority.[14]

Montessori education not only works along the lines proposed in Bruner's report, but it makes certain contributions that are more far-reaching. Therefore, I suggest that the research proposed in *The Process of Education* should certainly include a serious study of Montessori education and its application in the school.

NOTES

1. Helena A. Miller, "A Proposal for the Improvement of Education in America," *The American Biology Teacher*, vol. 27, no. 1 (January 1965).

2. E. C. Frijling-Schreuder, "Thoughts on Education," a paper read to the Dutch Psychoanalytical Society, Amsterdam, February 5, 1970.

3. Jerome S. Bruner, *Toward a Theory of Instruction* (Cambridge, Mass.: Belknap, Harvard University Press, 1966), p. 5.

4. Jerome S. Bruner, *The Process of Education* (Cambridge, Mass.: Harvard University Press, 1966).

5. In *The Challenge of Incompetence and Poverty* (Urbana: University of Illinois, 1969), pp. 2–3.

6. The Geneva school generally refers to Jean Piaget, Bärbel Inhelder, and their associates at the Institute for Psychology and the International Center of Genetic Epistemology in Geneva, Switzerland. For similarities between their findings and Montessori education, see *Montessori: A Modern Approach* (New York: Schocken Books, 1971), pp. 23–26.–P. L.

7. The basic difference here lies in the concept "readiness for learning." The Geneva school emphasizes the maturational development of the child through the stages of preoperational, operational, and formal operational thinking. The child is considered "ready" to learn any subject at any age, providing it is approached on the right level.

Montessori also recognized maturational stages of development (the sensitive periods, which include physical, emotional, and cognitive development). She was less interested in defining these stages than in meeting the needs of the child which they represented. She did not consider whether a child was "ready" to learn any particular subject, but rather devised her materials solely to meet the recognizable needs of the child during the various sensitive periods. Therefore, the phrase "readiness for learning" is not used in Montessori education. The words "aiding the child's development in its sensitive periods" are.–P. L.

8. For an explanation of his method in doing this, see Jean Piaget, *Logic and Psychology* (New York: Basic Books, 1958).

9. Maria Montessori, *Pedagogical Anthropology* (New York: Stokes, 1913).

10. Bruner, *The Process of Education*, p. 20.

11. Ibid., p. 31.

12. Ibid., p. 65.

13. Ibid., p. 91.

14. Ibid., p. 80.

6 / EDUCATION IN A CHANGING WORLD

When we consider mankind as a whole, it seems apparent that it does not adapt easily to changes, even those it has brought about itself. Yet, man is proud of his free will, his freedom of choice, and his independence. He also has a greater capacity for adaptation than animals, as well as greater intelligence, which enables him to learn through experience. In practice, however, this is not so evident. Egocentricity, intolerance, prejudice, stubbornness, narrowmindedness, conformism, and intellectual and moral confusion are rampant the world over.

This state of affairs, in combination with the steadily accelerating technical progesss and the growing population concentration in new industrial areas, is certainly not favorable to a harmonious development of the personality. The struggle for life is clearly aggravated, and the tensions in interpersonal relationships have increased. Automation of labor is accompanied by ever-increasing specialization, which tends to preclude an overall view of the field one is working in. The individual pursues immediately attainable goals. Dedication to work is eroded by the lure of wages, which then become an end in themselves. Competition increases, and relationships become more superficial and casual. Bureaucracy increasingly restricts personal freedom, and man becomes a mere digit. This diminishes his sense of responsibility toward the community and its political structures. He becomes increasingly lonely.

Survival as a person in this turbulent and ever-changing world is so difficult that even man's capacity to love and give of himself seems to give way before the craving for power, opportunism, and hypocrisy. The old values and institutionalized patterns of behavior no longer provide adequate norms. Yet they are still clung to, and as a result there is growing discrepancy between conscious and unconscious motivations.

In 1946, in a lecture considered impressive at the time, though now perhaps largely forgotten, Maria Montessori described the impasse now threatening mankind.[1] She pointed out that we are living in a new world, a world constructed with wonderful rapidity in the past century through the cooperation of intelligent men and with the help of machines. This world was not consciously willed by man. He was, in fact, surprised by it. Nevertheless, humanity is now united by common interests, and its home is no longer a specific nation, but the whole planet. Formerly, the unity of men was only an ideal. Now, exterior developments are creating a real unity of material interests, and thus laying the groundwork for the realization of that spiritual ideal.

However, this surprising achievement does not seem to us to be a triumph. It seems, rather, to be an awesome menace because man's development has not kept pace with his technological progress. Man is not conscious of his changed position in the world around him and therefore continues to cherish all the prejudices ingrained in his soul during the course of history.

The need to help man toward a new consciousness of, and a new adaptation to, the world in which he lives, is evident. In our time, man, whether conqueror or conquered, is the slave of his own environment. Seldom, if ever before, has he reached such an extreme of impotence. We are all, today, living in insecurity and fear. We are in bondage, even though we are not willing to admit it, and therefore repeat the stereotyped refrain that we are for freedom and independence. Real freedom will only be possible when the balance between man and his environment has been restored; in other words, when man has developed new values and has a more complete mastery of his environment. Only then will he be able to break his self-made and useless bonds and develop a firm orientation in the new circumstances of his world.

Montessori presented these ideas in 1946. Today, it is all too evident how difficult it is for adults to change their views, let alone alter their way of life. It is only when one studies man's development that his capacity for adaptation and the flexibility of his mind become apparent. Children have special potentialities that enable them, through interaction with their environment, to achieve self-realization. They do this, first, by becoming one with their immediate environment. This unity enables them to achieve freedom within their world as adults. The basic patterns of their behavior and their basic attitudes toward themselves, other people, and their environment are all determined in this early period. In Montessori's words,

> Because man is born in different periods of history, to which he always has to adapt himself, it is imperative that his being must first of all receive and collect, until the foundation is laid for every specific adaptation to the specific environment of that historical moment in which he was born. Thus, the first year of life appears as a period of exceptional activity in which the whole environment is absorbed by the psyche. In the second year, the child approaches its physical completion; its movements become determinate. This proves plainly how, in accordance with the natural pattern of development, the movements are determined by the psychic life.[2]

However, children need the guidance of adults as well; their development into independent and mature personalities depends on their further education. It is a mistake to think that this development will happen of its own accord, or that the personality traits considered necessary for well-adjusted behavior within a community come into being only during adolescence. A long and indirect process of preparation is necessary before these traits become manifest. Personal experiences during early childhood determine the role they play in the mature personality, as well as how they are expressed.

Because the basic patterns of human behavior are not determined by heredity, as in the case of animals, children must build these up through their own activities. From the beginning, they strive to achieve their personal aims, but they are dependent for their realization on the possibilities provided by their environment.

Reality imposes restrictions on what can be accomplished, educators posit norms, social life prescribes specific rules of conduct, society expects various skills and knowledge of its members, and their own bodies have their demands.

Further, the pattern of development inherent in the formation of man and which intrinsically guides the individual toward maturity, must be considered. This is manifested in the form of inner needs, differing according to the level of maturation, that direct the personality toward specific objects, activities, and experiences necessary for healthy development and adaptation. These needs serve to maintain the balance between the psychosomatic unity of the person and his environment.

Professor A. A. Schneiders of Boston College calls all physiological and psychological inner needs of this kind the intrinsically determined motivating factors of human behavior. He also points out their fundamental importance to the harmonious development of personality.[3] The fact that so many different factors play a part in the development of the personality precludes the prevention of conflicts. This is not in itself harmful, provided solutions are sought that lead to a further integration and enlargement of consciousness.

Here, the aid of education is indispensable. For example, the striving for independence is a fundamental characteristic of man that manifests itself from early youth on, provided a child feels sufficiently secure. If too much, or too little, is asked of children in this respect, they make no attempt at independence. Their physical growth may continue, but as persons they remain dependent and uncertain, even as adults.

In a paper read some years ago to teachers of secondary schools, I discussed another aspect of this problem—the emergence of gangs and juvenile delinquency among teenagers who are left to their own devices as they advance toward independence. Neither their parents nor their schools seem to be able to give them the aid necessary for them to orient themselves in their world.[4] Some years ago, J. Edgar Hoover, the late head of the F.B.I., called the increasing number of juvenile delinquents dangerous to the future of the country. More recently, a report was published in England dealing with the increasing amount of venereal disease among teenagers and pinpointing the laxness and indifference of parents regarding the education of their children as a co-determining factor.

The attitude of parents toward their children in early youth, as well as during puberty, is unquestionably a very important factor in determining their future attitude toward themselves and their fellow human beings. The first phase of life is of special importance because it is then that the development of personality takes place in the unconscious and provides the basis on which further individuation takes place.

These insights come from the pioneering work of Sigmund Freud, whose theory of personality may be regarded as the most influential and comprehensive to date. Psychoanalysis has brought to light fundamental and previously unknown features of human development, and thus contributed considerably toward a better understanding of the unconscious dynamics inherent in the genesis of personality. The model constructed from it indicates both the continuity and the successive variety of the basic pattern of development. At the same time, it takes into account the psychological as well as the biological and sociological determinants of behavior. Psychoanalysis has not only established the influence of the infantile situation in the formation of character. It has also shown how obstinately the patterns of adaptation established at this early stage persist in the adult personality, even if they prove inadequate to cope with the adult's life situation.

The decisive role of infantile experiences and emotional reactions has been demonstrated again and again. It is, at present, accepted in the majority of the theories of personality, though there are sharp differences of opinion about the nature and interpretation of findings. The following views are quite generally accepted: One, the way in which a child experiences different methods of education and infant care has a lasting effect on its personality. Two, the feeling of insecurity and fear experienced by a baby when its need for food, comfort, security, or love is too strongly or abruptly frustrated has an especially unfavorable effect. It may result in a deeply ingrained attitude of distrust of other people and the world in general. Three, still more important is the parent–child relationship during the whole period of development, particularly the first three years.

I would like to discuss some of the most common problems in this regard and their consequences for the adult personality. Rejection of children may lead to uncertainty and self-devaluation, often accompanied by hostility, rebelliousness, or other negative behavior, or else to apathy and indifference in adult life. Their ability to give and receive love will always be problematic. Maternal overprotection, if indulgent, may lead to egoism, egocentricity, irresponsibility, and a reduced tolerance of frustration; if dominating, it may lead to submissiveness, awkwardness, a lack of initiative, and passive dependence. In both cases, a heightened ambivalence in relationships with the opposite sex is to be expected. Too strict discipline may stimulate a basic attitude either of conformism or of rebellion. Inconsistent or inadequate discipline may weaken a person's self-control and ability to reach decisions or confront normal difficulties. An authoritarian and intolerant attitude on the part of parents with regard to the behavior of their children generally increases feelings of guilt and conflicts of conscience, and there is a high probability that the children will develop into rigid personalities. The generally accepted theories of personality also take into account family relationships, the position of the child in the family, sibling rivalry, and the educational situation in general, all of which are held to influence the development of the personality.[5]

Many more examples could be given of the fact that modern psychology regards the adequate gratification of inner needs as indispensable to the optimal development of the personality. These needs are not only for food, rest, and affection, but also for stimulation, self-development, exploration, independence, and responsibility. There may be a difference of opinion about the way in which this gratification should come about, but its necessity for healthy development is accepted by all.

These views are wholly in accordance with Montessori principles. It would seem useful, then, for other educators to study these principles, regardless of eventual differences of opinion about their practical applications. The method is not in itself of particular importance. What is essential is the realization that education plays a fundamental role in the development of the personality. It it essential to give form, content, and direction to personal existence. This function of education can only be realized to a significant extent if educators are guided by the knowledge of the inner needs determining human development and the influence of unconscious education is taken into account.

In our time, especially in view of the necessity for collaborating in our construction of a peaceful nuclear age, we may not disregard our responsibility to educate our children properly. It is not an easy task, but one we must attempt. Although we live in a world of contradictions, it is, nevertheless, rapidly becoming a common world. As a result, we become involved in an ever-increasing number of social contests as we come into contact with views, customs, ways of life, and values that differ from our own. How can young people orient themselves in a world where they are being overwhelmed by incoherent impressions, artificial stimuli, threats of war, materialistic philosophies, and double standards of morals; when they are surrounded by adults who often do not understand them because they themselves cannot adjust to too rapid changes, who are too busy to be bothered, or who only emphasize the immaturity of the young without providing any constructive visions to guide them; when their most obvious sources of inspiration are television and the bizarre products of industries specializing in the juvenile market and appealing to the most superficial aspects of their still unstable selves?

It is not surprising that, on the threshold of adulthood, young people tend to shrink from responsible participation in this apparently chaotic reality, that they take refuge in a world of their own making, one that reflects their inexperience, their labile emotional life, and their immaturity. There is something demonstrative, even defiant, about this phenomenon, as if the young would like to say, "If you can't be bothered about us, we will assert ourselves in our own way." This often takes the form of a forced attempt at adulthood, even to bringing into the world children whom they are totally incapable of raising. In this way, they add to the increasing number of unbalanced people in our culture.

We have no right to dissociate ourselves from these phenomena, from "the youth of today." The difference between them and us resides not in their youth itself, but in the circumstances in which they are growing up. We, the adults, are responsible for these circumstances, and hence for their consequences. It is our duty to look for the means that will enable the adults of tomorrow to live in peace with themselves and their world.

Education will, in any case, have to devote itself to the development of world citizens. The conception of "cosmic education," which Montessori introduced on the occasion of the International Montessori Conference in Amsterdam in 1950, and which is discussed in Chapter 8, was intended as a contribution in this direction.

The idea found no acceptance then. Apparently, the time was not ripe for such a reform. Perhaps the present world situation is more conducive to it. The interdependence of nations is constantly increasing. The prosperity and adversity of one is reflected in the others, and the necessity of accepting the idea of a world community has become more obvious.

Those who are aware of this should give the coming generation both a vision of the common destiny of humanity and a more adequate preparation for active cooperation to further common interests. We have already shown that adults do not easily change their accustomed views and that man has been unable to keep pace with the too-rapid changes brought about by his own inventions. Only a minority are mature enough to use these inventions constructively. In general, our situation can be compared with that of an unbalanced child in possession of a loaded gun. In his pursuit of progress, man has ignored his own development.

Maria Montessori said on this subject that "man has not yet built the same spiritual defences which hygiene prescribes for the body; no scientific aid whatsoever has been given to help the adaptation to radically changed ways of life. While he is in command of the riches and power of the earth, man has neglected the supreme energy of his own intellect." [6] The accuracy of her words is well illustrated in the pithy, brilliant description Jacques Barzun gives of our democratic culture, particularly with respect to the degradation of the human intellect. [7]

It is, therefore, an urgent necessity that the emphasis in scientific thought not be only on the qualities of the objective world. Equal weight should be given to the study of forces determining subjective behavior, which are still largely unknown.

Hopefully, then, new ways of coping with our changing world in a more efficient way will be discovered.

The situation is complicated by the rapidity with which the human sciences have developed and branched out. Because of this, they possess few certainties. At the same time, certainties are demanded in increasing measure by society. Scientists are thus put under pressure. They have to behave as authorities while being daily confronted by the insufficiency of their knowledge concerning their objects of study.

Man is not so easily fathomed. Not only are there many determinants to his behavior, but the vagueness and fluidity of his psychic life and the elusiveness of the spiritual aspect of his being make scientific research difficult. There is also the lack of distance between subject and object (which in this case coincide) to contend with. It is not mere chance that it took the empirical sciences so long to turn to the study of man's inner life.

Perhaps partly because of the speed with which this development did take place in the past decades, we find within this vast field of activity much the same situation as that in society in general. Increasing specialization has made it difficult for scientists to obtain an overall view of their own fields of study. As a result, they are inclined to retire to their own small area of experience and to ignore or vehemently combat their neighbors' findings. Because of this, their work often lacks an integrative purpose. They seem like drifting boats in the ever-increasing stream of practical problems. Sometimes they collide with one another; sometimes they are aided by another's wake. Actually, they lead nowhere. The general impression is often one of pseudo-science.

This unsatisfactory state of affairs makes the need for integration obvious. A growing number of scientists are becoming conscious of the common destiny of their efforts. Consequently, a willingness to cooperate to create "a comprehensive science of man" [8] is becoming apparent. Partly because of poor communication, this cooperation is only laboriously coming about. Actually, not much of it is evident, as yet. This is true even in particular disciplines and subdisciplines. It is also true in education, and for that matter in developmental psychology, which is no more than an umbrella for a large variety of views and findings. [9]

I have pointed out that Montessori's vision of man is the most valuable and scientifically fruitful aspect of her spiritual heritage. I believe that it is a useful point of departure for a new, comprehensive study of man. In it we may find a catalyst for the kind of cooperation mentioned above, particularly in the service of education. In my opinion, the study of man should primarily be concerned with man in infancy, when his existence is marked by seeming helplessness, but when he is actually involved in a potent inner activity. The essence of what is created by this inner activity eludes us. Nevertheless, it is of greater significance than all man's later creative achievements.

In infancy, the human being possesses specific potentialities whose nature is unknown to us, but whose effects have struck many scientists. The discoveries of Maria Montessori and Sigmund Freud have contributed greatly to our understanding of man at this early stage of development. Freud studied unconscious drives and their manifestations in emotionally disturbed adults within a special therapeutic situation; Montessori studied the manifest behavior of normal children in a specially prepared pedagogical situation. Both sought to explain the phenomena they observed, and both found general patterns in the development of the human being. In essence, these seem to confirm and to complement each other.

Psychoanalytic thought has undergone, in later years, a shift toward the consideration of normal development. Since this was the starting point of Montessori education, greater collaboration between the two disciplines may be conceivable in the future. In any event, they do have many principles in common. We should start from these, and adapt our educational aims to the basic patterns of development found. We will then be giving education a wider scope, that of helping in the formation of man. We should do this from the very beginning of life. Some will think that this way will take too long to be of any practical use in the solution of the problems confronting education today. We should remember, however, that the stimulus for our present technical progress was not the study of the macrocosmos. It was the study of the microcosmos, of particles too minute even to be seen.

The forces within the atom, for so long unknown to man, appear to be so potent that they will enable him to visit other planets, or to destroy himself entirely. Is it, then, so strange to assume that the study of the still mysterious forces of the mind, which enable the young child to construct within itself the foundations of its personal existence, may reveal things beneficial to man's development? I do not think so. Nor did Maria Montessori, or for that matter many others.[10]

In my opinion, education can only help to solve the present impasse in human affairs if it abandons its traditional preoccupation with the teaching of skills and the transfer of knowledge. Its goal should be, instead, to aid the basic patterns that direct man from within, so that balanced development can take place. Only in this way can modern man develop a personality flexible and strong enough to cope with the complex requirements of a rapidly changing world.

NOTES

1. Dr. Montessori was speaking to a congress organized by the Dutch branch of the New Education Fellowship, the Institute of Child Care and Education, and the Dutch Montessori Society in Utrecht. Her topic was "The Family."

2. Maria Montessori, *Aan de basis van het leven* (Bussum, Netherlands: Van Holkema en Warendorf, 1949), p. 86.

3. See A. A. Schneiders, *Personality Development and Adjustment in Adolescence* (Milwaukee, Wis.: Bruce, 1960).

4. M. M. Montessori, "Gedragsmotivatie bij de opgroeiende mens," a paper read to the principals and lecturers of the Montessori lycea, The Hague, February 28, 1964.

5. A very lucid exposition of the psychoanalytic viewpoint on assessments of development is given by Anna Freud in *Normality and Pathology in Childhood: Assessments of Development* (New York: International Universities Press, 1966).

6. See note 1 above.

7. Jacques Barzun, *The House of Intellect* (New York: Harper & Brothers, 1959).

8. C. Kluckhohn, *Mirror for Man* (New York: McGraw-Hill, 1949), p. 1.

9. M. M. Montessori, *Some Remarks on the Anthropology of Montessori Education* (Amsterdam: A.M.I. Communications, 1965).

10. See, for example, Rene A. Spitz and Godfrey W. Cobliner, *First*

Year of Life: A Psychoanalytic Study of Normal and Deviant Development of Object Relations (New York: International Universities Press, 1966).

7 / MONTESSORI AND THE REVOLUTION IN VALUES

As long ago as the 1940s, Maria Montessori was aware of the social crisis confronting us today. She described in powerful language human helplessness in the face of the forces of progress. Man himself, she wrote, had unchained these forces by his own creative action, but he had not been able to keep pace with them in terms of adaptation and development. There was "a lack of balance between man and his environment from which humanity must deliver itself by strengthening its own resources, developing its own values, healing its own madness, and becoming conscious of its own power." [1]

Little has been done, as yet, to correct this imbalance. On the contrary, not only does the situation seem to have deteriorated, but predictions for the near future are not at all reassuring. Professor Zbigniew Brzezinski of Columbia University foresees, for example,

A society culturally, psychologically, socially, and economically shaped by the impact of technology and electronics, with computers able to produce "creative" thought and, if wedded to robots, human-like action.

Human conduct itself being increasingly subjected to deliberate "programming," extensive chemical mind-control and [a] loss of individuality.

Atomized social life, increasingly purposeless masses in an amuse-
ment-focused society, [and] active work being the privilege of the
governing meritocratic elite.[2]

Brzezinski is aware of the potential dangers of such a world.
However, he also suggests that the capacity of government to assert
social and political control over the individual will vastly increase
and that this in its turn may encourage a technocratic dictatorship
in the next several decades. He points out several factors that allow
at least some optimism about such a society's capacity to meet the
challenge of the future.

This hope, however, is diluted by his concluding remarks on the
impact confrontation with a new technetronic society will probably
have on the world at large. Some local wars may occur, he argues,
resulting perhaps in the total nuclear destruction of one or several
smaller nations before the universal moral shock generated by the
destruction results in the imposition of greater international
controls.

The possibility of avoiding this catastrophe seems to him
remote. The instantaneous character of the electronic intermeshing
of mankind will create intense confrontations that will strain social
and international peace. The resulting trauma may create entirely
different perspectives on life, with insecurity, envy, and hostility
becoming the dominant emotions of increasingly large numbers of
people. Brzezinski mentions in this connection a three-way split
into rural-backward, urban-industrial, and technetronic ways of life.
Such a restructuring of society would further divide man, and
increase the obstacles to global understanding. He also remarks that
the rest of the world can learn what is in store for it by observing
what happens in the United States—not a very reassuring prospect.

I would like to point out a fourth disruptive factor if the
developments Brzezinski foresees take place. He mentions as one of
the positive features of the technetronic age the expansion of
knowledge and the entry into sociopolitical life of the intellectual
community. In the United States, though many urban dwellers
may be college trained, only a minority of them will belong to the
privileged meritocratic elite. The majority will form part of the
purposeless masses described earlier, who enjoy a longer lifespan

and a large amount of leisure. Presumably, the selection of the elite will be by computer. This may result in a subtler, but far more devastating, form of discrimination than that which causes us so much concern today. The college-trained citizens judged unfit for admission into the elite will, nonetheless, have been taught to think and to act intelligently. It is inconceivable that they will accept, for long, being branded as second-grade citizens by machines. Because they will still be human beings, a major revolt will probably occur, perhaps disrupting the whole system.

Brzezinski states that increasing attention must be given to improving the quality of life for man as man. It seems to me that this is the most urgent issue of our time. The situation of man, trapped by his environment, can be described by the following metaphor: God created man in His image, and man created machines in his image. The machines are now reshaping man, and God has been declared dead. The guiding and unifying principle in human existence has been eliminated. The individual is being deprived of his share in shaping his personal destiny. His life is being determined, more and more, by impersonal institutions and technological devices that keep him in bondage. Meaning and identity are being lost in the process. Anxiety and a growing feeling of disorientation, futility, helplessness, and frustration are taking over. In the circumstances, revolt is the only way the individual can recover his rights as a man.

We must keep in mind that when we speak of revolutions, whether they involve technology, social values, or political ideologies, we are always speaking of man and his behavior. I will clarify this point later. It is important to remember here that whatever conception of inner or outer reality we have, whatever values we possess or whatever meaning we attach to life, we are always dealing with psychic entities, and hence with subjective propensities. No matter how "objective" the outcome of a situation may seem to be, the human personality is involved.

However, because the educational and scientific establishment has mistakenly concluded that it is dealing with an objective situation, it has cultivated in its students only those faculties that have an objective purpose, leaving the development of the other aspects of the personality in abeyance. Technological progress has contributed this pragmatic and one-sided approach to education, demanding increasing specialization, and hence an increasing fragmentation of knowledge. At the same time, its very extent is shaking the basis of science, modern man's last hope of security.

Actually, man should find security within himself, but he has received no aid in developing his own resources to this end. Reason having failed as a source of stability, the exacting conformity required by modern technology becomes an insufferable and senseless burden, tolerated only for the material profit and social status it offers. Many cannot stand the strain and want to throw all rules and regulations overboard. They indulge in irrational ways of life, in which subjective feelings are the only things that count.

It is not accidental that the human sciences have developed so rapidly. Paradoxically, they have helped to increase our confusion. Having been modeled on the natural sciences and mathematics, they have adopted their perspectives and methods. They conceive of man as a machine, thereby serving the very system from which he is trying to escape. And to what avail? As Godfrey Cobliner puts it, "From the worship of authority we have shifted to the worship of the collectivity. Instead of acquiring diversity, we have drifted into conformity." [3] It becomes more and more difficult for modern man to find appropriate criteria to evaluate behavior. Standards tend to be considered more as styles that are "in" in certain groups and rejected in others, and have no special validity per se. What seems most dominant is confusion—particularly in the realm of values.

In view of this, it is my opinion that one cannot speak of revolution in this connection. Revolution implies having new values for which old ones must make way. We are far from this yet. There is no doubt that the rapid environmental changes of which we have spoken, with their emphasis on the material aspects of human existence, have their impact on our value system. However, environmental influences are only one side of the coin. Values are the result of an intricate process of development of the individual personality, by which interactions with the outer world are replaced by inner representations.

This process of internalization—of which the maturation of early ego functions is a precondition—has different stages. It starts with imitation, identification, and introjection with regard to the attitudes of parents and other significant persons in the child's environment. It culminates in the individual's views, ideals, and standards, as evidenced by his behavior and his role in the society in which he lives.[4] This is what is understood by his ego identity. It is usually considered to be achieved developmentally during the normative crisis of adolescence. However, if the environment is suitably benign, the maturation of specific ego functions continues to occur in the normal individual well into adult life. It is evidenced by a steadily increasing capacity to love, to work, and to adapt to the world.

This does not happen in circumstances that cause anxiety. Generally speaking, what we see then is a backward movement, or regression, to more primitive and infantile emotional responses. Anna Freud remarks that the normal citizen does not internalize the law as such. Rather, his attitude toward it perpetualizes "the infantile position of an ignorant and compliant child, faced by parents who are omniscient and omnipotent. The delinquent or criminal perpetuates the attitude of the child who ignores, or belittles, or disregards parental authority, and acts in defiance of it."[5] The same phenomenon can occur with regard to the social system as a whole when it is too coercive. In my opinion, this is also the cause of the existing confusion in values. When freedom is confused with license,[6] adaptation with conformism,[7] discipline with submissiveness,[8] independence with antiauthoritarianism,[9] equality with uniformity,[10] and so forth, we are dealing with an infantile attitude to the social system. It had its beginnings in the child's reaction to an omnipotent and, I may add, intolerant parent. It is clear that those who harbor these misconceptions will also be motivated by them.

More specific value distortions are those related to primitive defense mechanisms, activated by the regressive phenomenon mentioned above. These can be seen, for example, in a rigid adherence to a specific value system maintained by denying those aspects of reality that cause anxiety, guilt, or pain. This rigidity is generally compensated for by a fantasy of omnipotence.

In still another form of value distortion, those aspects of reality that are felt to be the most disruptive elements of the governing social system are adopted as personal values to be adhered to and propagated with the determination of a crusader. This is achieved by a combination of primitive defense mechanism.[11] We then see, for example, change being considered a guiding principle in its own right. Everything must be continuously changed whether it makes sense or not. In fact, of course, change is a neutral concept. It can lead equally to improvements or to disasters. The same can be said of speed, research, techniques, systems, procedures, action; all these and many more similar means are dissociated from the aims they should serve. They are promoted to the status of autonomous values, and thereby lose their purpose. Consider the rage for innovation. How well we are all acquainted with it!

This brings us to the conflict between generations. The following observations give the gist of the situation:

> An excessive desire for liberty at the expense of everything else is what undermines democracy and leads to the demand of tyranny . . . it will permeate private life . . . it becomes the thing for father and son to change places, the father standing in awe of his son, and the son neither respecting nor fearing his parents, in order to assert his independence. . . . The teacher fears and panders to his pupils, who in turn despise their teachers and attendants; and the young as a whole imitate their elders, argue with them and set themselves up against them, while their elders try to avoid the reputation of being disagreeable or strict by aping the young and mixing with them on terms of easy good fellowship.[12]

These words could easily apply to certain aspects of today's social turbulence. They were, however, written by Plato some four centuries before the birth of Christ. I do not quote him with the intention of downgrading the present problems between generations, but to put them in the right perspective—to show that although times, conditions, and interpretations change, there is something basic determining human behavior that does not. I will come back to this point later.

A better understanding of modern youth and its problems calls for a consideration of some general points. First of all, we should acknowledge the fact that the impact of World War II on those of us who were young at the time was much more profound and disturbing than we generally care to admit. It undoubtedly had repercussions on the way we brought up our children. Often, covering our insecurity as educators by calling ourselves modern or progressive, we gave them a more permissive education than we received. More often than not, we neglected our true responsibility in respect to what Hannah Arendt calls the double aspect of childhood: that of being newcomers in a strange world and unfinished beings in the process of becoming.[13] We offered them more material advantages that allowed them to enter the adult world earlier, but we did not give them a meaningful perspective on it. Their most direct preparation for the world at large was the kaleidoscopic explosion of images by which television brings its inconsistencies home to us. The poet A. E. Housman describes well what the young must feel on encountering the adult world:

> I, a stranger and afraid,
> In a world I never made.[14]

A second thing we must consider is that when we speak of youth, or the younger generation, we are making a single entity of something that is not. The only thing young people have in common, and that only within a broad margin that should be specified in talking about them, is their position in the continuum of human life from birth to death. That we can talk about such an abstraction as youth at all is evidence that there is an intrinsic pattern determining human development. It manifests itself in a specific way and gives a special quality to the behavior of a group of peers. However, the individuals in that peer group differ, as all human beings do. Furthermore, individuals can only be considered in relation to all other members of the communities in which they grow and live, and to the environment at large.

Now, the great majority of modern youth neither rebels against society, nor withdraws from it. They do look at it critically and realistically, with a great deal of insight and understanding. In addition, what they demand from adults is fully reasonable. They wish to be treated as fellow human beings in their own right. It is in this sense that they request equality. They know very well that they lack experience, and they are willing to learn; but they do not want to take things for granted. They want to participate in what goes on and, at the very least, be informed of the motives behind decisions that influence their existence. They are all too aware that they will presently have to find their place and function independently in a world of which they know themselves to be citizens, but which appears, on the surface at least, to be a thoroughly chaotic place. They are not prepared to accept any of the roles they are offered by society uncritically. In addition, they will keep their inner reserve until they are quite sure of their choice. Any genuine help their elders can give them in this connection will be sincerely appreciated.

This is why we do great injustice to our children when we speak of them as part of "modern youth" instead of as individual human beings, especially if we identify them a priori with one of the minorities that receive attention because they happen to be in conflict with society. We then force them to assume that role, whether we are conscious of it or not. In fact, rebellion against or withdrawal from society is an extreme reaction that occurs only when circumstances cause intolerable tensions in interpersonal relationships. It occurs, for example, where a pocket of poverty exists in an otherwise affluent society, where housing problems preclude a livable environment, where a minority is discriminated against for some reason, or in the case of students, where the situation is complicated by a system that is the most conservative ever to exist, and which by tradition requires that one endure willingly.

Of course, in these cases a typological generalization of youth also does a further injustice to the individuals concerned. Not only does it highlight only one side of the picture, but it ignores the fact that there are great differences in individual motivations, which may range from sincere convictions and a wish for a more livable community to pure destructiveness.

However, because of their damaging effect, some general behavior patterns should be considered that lead to the phenomenon generally called the generation gap. When young people have genuine grievances that are not taken seriously by the authorities, they protest; they seek support from others in similar circumstances.

Pearl King, in a study of racial prejudice, describes aptly what happens next.[15] When an individual starts to behave contrary to our expectations, it generally arouses unconscious anxiety, aggression, and guilt feelings. As a result, we tend to categorize actions as typical of an existing stereotype such as "youth," "the poor," or "blacks." Stereotyped beliefs develop that are mistaken, in whole or in part, for established facts.

The person against whom this type of prejudice is directed has no way of escape. The resulting stress leads to a regression to more primitive forms of social and interpersonal behavior. When individuals function even partly in this way, they begin to treat others as inanimate objects devoid of human feelings. The span of time over which they feel responsibility for their actions shrinks, so that the consequences are felt to be the responsibility of others. Morality deteriorates to the law of Talion: Who does not agree is an enemy. Their world and their relationships are experienced in terms of opposites: as all black or all white, all good or all bad. They desperately need a person or group to blame as the source of every discomfort and evil in order to maintain some degree of psychic equilibrium. Their chief defenses or methods of adaptation are projection, splitting, and denial. They create stereotyped images onto which they can project all those aspects of themselves that are not congruent with their preferred self-image. Such stereotyped images can be communicated quickly through normal communication channels and, with the aid of modern propaganda techniques, can rapidly become widespread.

King's remarks shed a great deal of light on the processes underlying what is commonly called the generation gap. These processes are operative among both the young and the representatives of the establishment. They reinforce the initial distrust and hostility between the two, thus precluding the possibility of a genuine dialogue.

This is a complex picture, but such is the human situation. What can we deduce from it? One thing is certainly clear. From whatever angle we look at it, we are always brought back to the individual human being, his development, and his behavior. This appears to be the basic issue, to which all others are related. We cannot avoid the fact, either, that the transition to a postindustrial society is creating a serious human crisis that could easily get out of hand. Clearly, all those who have chosen as their profession the study or guidance of human beings must coordinate their efforts to achieve systematically planned objectives. Only in this way can they help to reduce the existing confusion regarding values, and to reorient man with regard to his position and role in handling his affairs.

We have called for concerted action based on a firm common body of knowledge concerning man and his behavior. We have discussed the problems involved. The realm of science is not any freer from prejudices, struggles, and contradictions than any other sector of human activity. The situation is particularly confused when we study man because of his complexity, on the one hand, and his great subjectivity on the other. The combination of these two factors often leads to oversimplification. If modern science has taught us anything, it is that truth is elusive and that no one approach leads to it. The best we can do is converge on it from several perspectives.

In the human sciences, this is only possible if a consensus can be reached on a general scheme. This scheme should serve as a matrix for integrating the findings obtained by different approaches. It should include and explain all aspects of man's development, his behavior, and his relations to others and to his environment at large as they really are. This means that a coherent network of propositions concerning the human personality as an entity must be constructed.

The latter can be seen as evolving in interaction with the environment, passing through distinct stages of development and leading to ever more complex behavior. This conception acknowledges the complexity of the human being and his behavior in different situations and cultures. Through such a conception, the findings of all those studying his behavior from different approaches can be coordinated into a comprehensive picture that will fit the requirements of science. It is the only conception of man that can be of any real help in finding adequate solutions for the social problems we have been discussing.

This concept is of particular importance in connection with education. One of the most persistent prejudices in the realm of human sciences is that against the child. Its fundamental function in the formation of man continues to go unrecognized, although

Maria Montessori began discussing her discoveries in this field in 1912. Her observations of the child revealed that characteristics related to the value system were developed through spontaneous activity in a prepared environment. Adults must help the child to function freely in this environment. This help corresponds to the intrinsic needs inherent to the pattern of development, and follows his own tempo. Montessori demonstrated that under these conditions the child is urged from within towards certain specific activities which he performs with great concentration and joy. These activities are linked to the inner formation of functions that only later are integrated and appear as manifest characteristics.

The goal of Montessori education is the formation of the child's whole personality. In the beginning, the child works mainly independently, but it observes what others around it do, especially the older children. Presently, it starts to collaborate with others. The older children participate in the activities of younger ones and help them in a natural way that both enjoy. Instead of competitiveness, there is cooperation. This enhances the children's feeling of security and stimulates them to further exploration of their world. Respect for others and for the environment comes as a natural byproduct of the freedom within a community they experience.

It is interesting to note that several of the characteristics so often exhibited in Montessori schools are considered basic to human welfare and development by social scientists. In a list of properties of biosocial and sociocultural systems, Eric Trist mentions self-regulation, integration, independence, interdependence, coordination, and cooperation as basic to welfare and maturation, learning extended adaptability, the accumulation of culture, and expansion of the environment.[16] Because these are all properties that are explicitly encouraged by Montessori education, it certainly deserves serious consideration in the search for the best means to prepare tomorrow's citizens. As Montessori wrote in her last book,

> One of the most urgent endeavors to be undertaken on behalf of the reconstruction of society is the reconstruction of education [to awaken] those marvellous powers which today remain hidden. . . . Then there will appear the child who is destined to form a humanity capable of understanding and controlling our present civilization.[17]

NOTES

1. Maria Montessori, *The Formation of Man* (Adyar, India: Kalakshetra, 1955).

2. Zbigniew Brzezinski, "America in the Technetronic Age," *Encounter* (January 1968), pp. 16–26.

3. Godfrey Cobliner, quoted in Rene A. Spitz, *The First Year of Life* (New York: International Universities Press, 1965), app., p. 365.

4. For a detailed exposition of this intricate process of development, see Anna Freud, *Normality and Pathology in Childhood* (New York: International Universities Press, 1966), pp. 170–84.

5. Ibid., p. 183.

6. See F. J. J. Buytendijk, *Experienced Freedom and Moral Freedom in the Child's Conscience* (Amsterdam: A.M.I. Communications, 1963).

7. See Jeanne Lampl-deGroot, "Some Thoughts on Adaptation and Conformism," a psychoanalytic study distinguishing between adaptive and conforming behavior, in R. M. Loewenstein et al., eds., *Psychoanalysis—A General Psychology* (New York: International Universities Press, 1966).

8. See Aldous Huxley, *Ends and Means* (New York: Harper & Brothers, 1937), pp. 200f., in which he quotes Maria Montessori on this subject and discusses the coexistence of education for freedom and responsibility and education for bullying and subordination in Western democracies.

9. See Hannah Arendt, *Between Past and Future* (New York: Meridian Books, 1963), pp. 190f.

10. Ibid., p. 180.

11. For a better understanding of these mechanisms, see Anna Freud, *The Ego and the Mechanisms of Defense*, rev. ed. (New York: International Universities Press, 1967).

12. Plato, *The Republic*, trans. H. D. P. Lee (Harmondsworth: Penguin Books, 1968), pp. 335–36.

13. Hannah Arendt, "The Crisis in Education," in *Between Past and Future* (New York: Meridian Books, 1961), pp. 173–97.

14. A E. Housman, *Last Poems* (Chester Springs, Pa.: Dufour, 1922).

15. Pearl H. M. Kin, "Exploring Racial Prejudice," a public lecture given in London, February 1970 (unpublished).

16. Eric L. Trist, "The Relation of Welfare and Development in the Transition to Post-Industrialism," in F. E. Emery and E.L. Trist, *Towards a Social Ecology: Contextual Appreciation of the Future in the Present* (New York: Plenum, 1970).

17. Maria Montessori, *The Formation of Man*, p. 98.

8 / COSMIC EDUCATION

One of the most fascinating characteristics of Maria Montessori was her ability to connect life at the moment with life in the distant past. A simple task would start her sketching a panoramic vision of man's evolution up to the present time, irresistably stimulating the imagination of her listeners.

I remember her peeling potatoes and looking at them with profundity, as if they could reveal some secret of great importance. She continued her task, wondering aloud how man originally discovered the value of the potato plant, outwardly a weed with insignificant little flowers and producing poisonous fruit. What made him look further? By what trick of chance did he discover that its usefulness to him lay not in the part of it that appeared above the surface, but in the part that was hidden in the earth? How did he learn that this part was not poisonous, but edible? Potato plants apparently came from the New World. How had they come to be introduced, adopted, and cultivated throughout Western Europe?

The way she could talk about things like potatoes brought one immediately to a higher level of thinking and view of reality, while, at the same time, one remained immersed in human life. It was a unique experience. It was connected with a special quality of her personality and a profundity of insight fundamental to her success.

Although she may not have made the connection consciously

herself, I believe her development of cosmic education grew out of this unusual ability to connect the past and the present through imaginative thinking. As she herself has pointed out,

> Imaginative vision is quite different from mere perception of an object, for it has no limits. Not only can imagination travel through infinite space, but also through infinite time; we can go backwards through the epochs, and have the vision of the earth as it was, with the creatures that inhabited it. To make it clear whether or not a child has understood, we should see whether he can form a vision of it within the mind, whether he has gone beyond the level of mere understanding. . . . The secret of good teaching is to regard the child's intelligence as a fertile field in which seeds may be sown, to grow under the heat of flaming imagination. Our aim therefore is not merely to make the child understand, and still less to force him to memorize, but so to touch his imagination as to enthuse him to his inmost core.[1]

In general, we seem to make little use of our imaginative powers in worldly affairs. We are involved in a continuous cycle of chaos that eventually evolves into order only to lapse into chaos once more. Lately the impetus of this cycle seems to have increased. As a result, many of man's spiritual values are being prematurely destroyed. Changes are so violent and contain so much potential for destruction that it is questionable whether we will find the wisdom within ourselves to redirect the situation so that we move toward a more constructive future.

What impresses me most in reviewing the social situation is that we go randomly from one extreme to the other. Our attitude toward pollution is a good example. People had been talking about the dangers of pollution for decades. Nobody listened. Suddenly the message was heard; everyone became aware of poisons in the air and threats to wildlife. Something had to be done, and quick! Everyone demanded an immediate solution to the problem. Of course, this was not possible. Some short range measures were taken to stop the shouting. These had other consequences as destructive as the initial pollution.

In reviewing history, it does not appear that political systems in themselves are the answer to human problems. Rather, solutions seem to depend on certain human beings who happen to be in positions of responsibility, on their personalities and their vision, or lack of it. Others, sometimes silent and sometimes shouting, merely follow their lead. The individual personality must develop the independence and maturity needed to see the present situation clearly and to visualize the future. It will then be possible to consider the direction we are going and how to influence matters so that we, with our powers of adaptability, our intelligence, and our creativity, can find a constructive way to handle our world, a world which in itself is a beautiful place to live and which could be much more agreeable than it happens to be at the moment. This kind of independence and maturity, however, seems to be scarce.

I believe that Montessori education aids the development of these qualities and, in this sense, provides a more realistic basis for hope for the future. This is most readily apparent when one examines Montessori's concept of cosmic education. There are three separate aspects of this conception that should be considered in this regard. The first is the underlying conception of man and human development, particularly between six and fourteen years of age. The second is the role of education and how to find the appropriate way to help the children of this particular age group develop as they should. The third is the practical techniques to be used in the schools, the didactic aspect. As I am not a teacher, I shall limit my remarks to the first two aspects.

Recently I chanced to see a television documentary on the life cycle of the pink salmon. It was a report of one of Captain Jacques-Yves Cousteau's experiments with his oceanographic research vessel *Calypso*. The site was a lake in Alaska that had once contained a great quantity of pink salmon. However, salmon factories had been built around it, and eventually the salmon had been exterminated. The site had then been abandoned. What Cousteau had done was to place fertilized pink salmon eggs in this environment that had originally proved so propitious for harboring their kind.

The eggs, which had been fertilized in quite a different location, were brought in containers to the lake and left there to hatch. As a result, a new cycle of salmon life was started. The young salmon eventually went down to the open sea, where they remained for four to five years, and then returned to the lake where they had been hatched.

When one stops to think of it, it is very curious that these fish were prompted by an inner urge to abandon a rich and calm environment of sweet water to go down a turbulent river to the sea, to adapt to a salt-water environment, to remain there for years, and then, eventually, to come back—as if directed by some hidden device—to the spot where they were born. To return, they had, once again, to undergo a physiological adaptation, this time from salt-water life back to that of sweet water. To do this, they had to live for some time in the area where the river entered the sea, until this readjustment had been completed. Then they started the laborious journey up the stream. Many of the fish died in the process, dashing themselves against rocks or jumping too far from the river bed. All kinds of animals inhabited the shores of the river, feeding off the fish. Thus the environment was kept clean of decaying bodies. However, the majority of salmon remained alive. At a certain stage of the trip, the males chose mates, and fought off other males. The couples thus formed continued upstream to the lake, where the eggs were laid and fertilized. Soon after, the adult fish died and their bodies decomposed very quickly. The lake became a true cemetery of salmon, their decomposed bodies providing plankton for the next generation of salmon to feed on. When this next generation is grown, it too will travel seaward, and the life cycle of the salmon will continue.

What can we learn from this captivating story? First of all, it teaches an ecological lesson: the interrelation between different aspects of the natural environment. Second, it shows the very close relationshiop between living beings and their environment: their adaptation to its more rigid features and their contribution to maintaining the conditions necessary for the existence of their species. The latter is what Maria Montessori calls the cosmic task.

Her ultimate explanation of this task as a finality, intended by creation to maintain the cosmic order in nature, belongs to her personal philosophy and need not be accepted by all. But the phenomena to which she alludes in explaining it are observable and belong to the natural order of things. Today this is referred to as the natural equilibrium. Scientists remained blind to it for a long time, considering those few who pointed it out eccentrics.

One final thing we can learn from the history of Captain Cousteau's salmon is the difference in the instincts of animals and men, as well as the special position of the latter in the cosmos. Let me explain these different aspects belonging to the cosmic or natural order in contradistinction to the social order.

I shall not expand on the general interrelation of all the components of the natural environment, which would bring us too far afield. We know, however, that the original movements of the surface of our planet left recesses that retain fresh water produced by the cycle of evaporation and the condensation in the atmosphere. The resulting lakes divided into streams or rivers flowing toward the sea, creating a special environment for certain animals such as the pink salmon. By what whim of nature we do not know, but through slow changes in the interaction of this species and its environment, a detailed pattern of behavior became hereditary. We could call what happened a programming, covering in this case a period of some five years and comprising such contrasting elements that they seem to the superficial observer to be unnatural. One would expect that, once accustomed to sweet water, these animals would find any other environment unpleasant and hence to be avoided. But this is not what happens. On the contrary, they find an area where sweet water from the river and salt water from the sea meet and patiently remain there, slowly adapting to the new condition. They then go off in schools, seemingly forgetting their place of origin. They may wander quite far, finding new depths and meeting new dangers, yet feeling at home in their new environment. What happens then is quite incomprehensible, yet happen it does, with computerized precision.

The different schools of salmon, all of a sudden, and more or less at the same time, change their course toward their place of origin. They again remain in an estuary for the time necessary to readjust to sweet water, and then start their dramatic trip against the current to the protected environment in which they were born to lay their eggs. Their life cycle then completed, they die quickly, providing the environment with the substance most necessary for the new life to come.

The detailed way in which hereditary instinctual patterns can structure the behavior of animals, and the precise timing involved, is extraordinary. In humans, certain fundamental patterns and sequences of development are hereditary, but individual behavior is shaped through experience and interaction with the environment. Infants can be brought from one environment to another; they will adapt to the environment in which they grow up. This experience will form them into adult members of that particular community. They will then act as if their behavior was hereditary, like the instinctual behavior of the salmon. Being human beings, however, they have built up their behavior patterns, through education and with the aid of the other members of the community.

What makes Montessori education so special is that its objective is to help human beings with the enormous task of inner construction necessary to pass from childhood to full adulthood. Education is an essential aspect of human development. We cannot become fully adult without it. The level of formation the individual personality can reach depends on it.

Montessori education aims to further this formation of personality. It is, therefore, astonishing that so many people have the impression that it is only meant for small children. The Montessori approach can be applied from birth, and even before birth through the preparation of adults for parenthood, and Montessori education can be continued until a child reaches maturity. In Holland, secondary schools based on Montessori principles have been in existence since 1931.

To return to our theme, when a child has had the help it needs, an integration of the personality takes place in approximately the sixth year. This integration marks the end of a phase of life lived in a protected environment, during which the child was directly dependent on the adults responsible for taking care of it. During this period, basic behavioral patterns and attitudes were internalized and integrated into the child's personality. At the same time, a differentiation of sensorial experiences and an indirect preparation for new functions began developing.

At a certain moment, the child itself wishes to come out of its protective shell, and to explore the bigger world. Of course, emergence from a protected environment is relative, because it is not yet capable of really going out and about all by itself. However, one can notice its increasing independence from its parents. At this stage of development, one can observe a growing interest in the behavior of peers and the wish to join others in groups. In addition, adults other than parents are idealized. There is a marked tendency to identify with group heroes who serve as models. At this time, a new attitude toward the world clearly begins. Cosmic education offers the kind of help that will activate the new potentialities consolidated at this first level of integration. The stage has been set for this activation through indirect preparation in an earlier phase. All the experiences that were offered to the child previously in the prepared environment were basic experiences, needed either for the formation of later functions, or as keys to help it to explore and orient itself in its world. When it reaches this second stage of maturity, it should be given a broader view of that world; that is, a vision of the whole universe.

This is a different approach from the one usually found in schools. The idea, as mentioned above, is to try to awaken the imagination of the child, to give it a vision of the order of things. The inner order of the personality must be constructed through experiences in a structured world. Thus the child must have a coherent picture, on the broadest scale possible, of the ambience in which he is growing. Chaos will never stimulate it to real participation.

Inner order is necessary to be able to see meaning in one's existence, to find one's identity, to achieve independence, and to act in a meaningful way. Interest in special details is never activated without a prior interest in the whole. Generally, in elementary education one finds an endeavor to teach facts as clearly as possible, starting with the most simple and elementary and proceding to the more complex and abstract. The students find this boring and must force themselves to learn by an act of will. To arouse their interest, they must first be shown the interrelation of things in the world— the different aspects of knowledge that can be studied, how they relate to each other or how they have come about.

One way to give children the global view of the universe they need is by introducing the ecological principle in education. The interrelation of living and nonliving things can be considered—what plants, for example, need from the earth to be able to grow, what special functions they have with regard to carbon dioxide, oxygen, water, and so on. Or the story of the pink salmon can be told in an interesting way that appeals to the imagination of the listeners. Different aspects of their life cycle can be introduced that arouse curiosity and that subsequently can be studied in detail by the children. They will do this with pleasure, because one of the normal traits of a happy human being is its desire to use its intelligence and endless curiosity to know, to explore, and to discover new things or new ways to use familiar things.

It is to this trait that education must appeal. Learning should not be an effort for children, a burden, or a tedious duty performed for the sake of the approval of someone in authority. On the contrary, it should result from a personal interest and involvement in the world, and an understanding of the meaning of things. When it does, a child is able to orient itself with regard to society, to the history of man, and to the future. If children are under six, history, for instance, can be taught in a way that helps them to determine their own identity by knowing how others lived in the past and in other cultures. However, what interests older children far more is a broader view of man: when he appeared on earth and how he evolved through the centuries. The idea then is to give a dynamic global view of how human life on earth has evolved, eventually forming what Maria Montessori called the "Supra Nature."

Children at this stage are fascinated because this story concerns them personally. They are beginning to be aware of their own situation as developing human beings. It also makes them conscious in a natural way of the difference between man and other living beings. There is an interrelationship between both and the environment. This interrelationship is evident in what Maria Montessori referred to as the cosmic task—the service that must be rendered by the individuals of each species to the environment on which they are dependent for their existence to maintain it in such a way that it will support their descendents, generation after generation. Some do this through their death, like the salmon whose decaying bodies provide plankton for their young. Others do it during their lifespan. Bees, for example, need flowers so that they can gather nectar to make honey. One might call this their main concern, if one could credit them with consciousness. During this process they inadvertently fertilize the flowers they visit by carrying pollen from one to another on their hairy legs. In this way they not only make use of the environment, but they preserve and cultivate that part of it which is needed for the survival of their species.

Man's interrelationship with the environment is different, however. He is an agent of change. He does not have the same fixed correlation with the environment as animals. He has the urge not only to adapt to the environment, but to change it as he goes along and as his needs and his imagination (or lack of it) dictate. This is what Maria Montessori called the cosmic task of man: to continue the work of creation.

Ever since his appearance on earth, man has continued changing and enriching his environment. Man has the power to create fantastic new possibilities. He may travel to other planets, or totally destroy this one. His power needs guidance. Bees, needing nectar, also see to the fertilization of the local flowers. Humans, needing salmon, fish for it in an area until it is exterminated, and then go elsewhere. It would have been quite easy to avoid destroying all the salmon in the Alaskan lake described earlier. And it would have been in the fisheries' interest to have done so. However, the vision for such long-range planning was lacking. Man does not have inbuilt programming, as does the salmon. He must program himself, through conscious effort. It is obvious today that man desperately needs the intelligence to use his power to change things constructively. This is his only hope, if he is to maintain his self-made environment in a condition that may permit human life to evolve toward a dignified existence for everyone. This can only be achieved with the aid of education.

It is important, then, to realize that the real aim of Montessori education is not the imparting of knowledge for the sake of learning itself. Rather, it encourages learning because learning is a feature of human development, a need that cannot be met without education. Consequently, it is first necessary to study human development and to gain insight into the special needs of the growing individual in different phases of his life.

By special needs I do not mean what John, or Mary, or another child wishes at a particular moment, but the inner needs that guide the development of the individual personality. An adult who wants to help growing individuals with this great task of construction must understand the multiplicity of factors determining human behavior and their relationship to the developmental profile of human life.

Historically, the complexity of this process has not really been taken into consideration in connection with education. Lately, however, its relevance is becoming more and more understood, particularly at higher levels of education. Universities and high schools are beginning to understand how much the effectiveness of their work depends on what their students have been able to achieve within themselves during the preceding period. There is more understanding of human development as a continuous process in which the individual remains the same psychosomatic entity while constantly adapting to changes in his environment. It is, then, not so important which facts one teaches the student, because very often these facts are already obsolete by the time they can be used. It is more important to help him to develop his potentialities so that he can rely on his own ability to cope with the unexpected and solve whatever new problems may crop up. In other words, he must be helped to feel independent in his own world and to develop the vision that will help him as an adult to maintain the environment in such a way that the unending, creative, and gigantic cosmic task of man can continue.

The common intelligence we all share has, for all practical purposes, no limits. Man can go on finding new possibilities forever. It is to this common intelligence, a dynamic communal entity that is created by the individual personalities forming the community, that cosmic education is directed. The progress, or lack of it, of the human community is determined by the concerted action of the individuals in it. If we merely react to ad hoc happenings and crises, our progress will be poor and our actions will be shortsighted. If we are inspired by vision and creative imagination, our progress can be very great and our actions future oriented. Cosmic education seeks to offer the young, at the appropriate sensitive period, the stimulation and help they need to develop their minds, their vision, and their creative power, whatever the level or range of their personal contributions may be.

NOTE

1. Maria Montessori, *To Educate the Human Potential* (Adyar, India: Kalakshetra, 1948), pp. 14–15.

APPENDIX:
A MONTESSORI
CLASSROOM
Paula Polk Lillard

It is difficult to develop a feel for Montessori education until it can be experienced as an ongoing involvement with children. The following scenes from a Montessori classroom are presented for those who are unfamiliar with the Montessori approach in action.

At eight-thirty, there are six or seven children out of a possible twenty or so already in the room. They are three to six years old, but I am surprised at how tiny several of them seem.

I am aware first of two boys sitting opposite each other on a small rug on the floor. I call them A and B for convenience. There is a basket of solid geometric shapes (wooden ones, smooth and shiney with a blue enamel paint) between them. A is blindfolded. He is turning one of the solids over in his hands. "You're peeking! Can't peek!" Says B, who is not blindfolded. "I feel it," says A, rolling it carefully between his hands. "What is it?" "Ovoid" answers B. A takes off the blindfold and looks. "Right," he says. Now B takes a solid. He has apparently decided to dispense with the blindfold and has simply closed his eyes. "Ellipsoid," he says. A, with the blindfold still pushed up, says, "No. Sphere." "Sphere," B repeats. A little girl who has stopped to watch says "sphere," pronouncing the "sp" distinctly; then she moves on, watching me a bit. B now picks up another solid. "What is it?" he asks. "Cylinder," says A. "Okay." B takes another object. "Cone," he suggests. "No," A tells him, "triangular prism." Both boys are having a fine time. I sense no competitive feelings, but there is a good deal of teaching going on as one names objects for the other. A says, "I'll make a house." I expect a switch to dramatic play, but A takes a triangular-based prism and places it on a rectangular-based prism, making what looks like a house with a roof. "Oh yeah," says B.

A little girl standing by me says, "See that lady in the red shirt and pants in the hall? That's my mother." She sits down at the table next to me, which has bells on wooden stands on two shelves. She begins to sound them with a small mallet, moving up and down the scale. She stops the sounds with a felt stopper similar to the mallet.

I notice the chart behind her on the wall at the height of "small people's" eyes. It's an ecology chart. It says "Save our parks. Save our birds. Save our air." There is an attractive picture under each saying. It is quite simple and easy to see from a distance. It is the only printed material hung on the walls of the room. In fact, I now notice that the walls of the room are largely blank. There are only two other objects on them. One is a mural behind me which the children have made. It is of animals, plants, and birds. The other is opposite me: a montage of the sun, earth, and stars in colored paper showing the simple relationship of each to the other, also made by the children.

I look at the room as a whole for the first time. Simplicity is its chief characteristic. The shelves (which are low and set along the walls) have many materials on them, but they appear uncluttered and carefully arranged. They are obviously divided into areas: one for materials used in practical life exercises (mostly small baskets containing various materials), one for sensorial materials (many in wooden boxes), one for academic materials, one for artistic materials. There are no colored tapes or marks to show the children where the different materials go. Even though they are very young, they obviously manage to remember.

I look about the room to see what's happening. I'm taking notes, and the little girl who stopped to watch the boys with the solids comes over to see my writing. She sighs, hands on hips, seeming a bit sleepy. Several other children are walking about, and some are working at tables. A girl watches a boy working on a puzzle map. She says, "I've got new shoes." "Oh," he replies. "Who bought those shoes for you?" She watches him for awhile and they talk a little more.

A tiny girl takes a furry animal out of a cage, holding it partly by the neck. I feel a little concern for them both. The teacher, whom I have not really been aware of as yet, speaks to her. The little girl then carries the animal carefully to the table, cradling it in her arms. She holds it up now and then—gently for such a little child— but I am glad the teacher has quietly spoken to her assistant, who appears to be staying nearby. The animal is one I am not familiar with—not a gerbil, hamster, or guinea pig. It washes its face with its paws and wanders quietly about the table top. After fifteen minutes or so, the little girl carries it safely back to its cage, and I breathe an apparently unnecessary sigh of relief.

The teacher now speaks quietly to the little girl who had watched me earlier. The girl goes and gets a tray, chooses a metal inset (a blue geometric shape in a red metal frame—in this case a circle), three colored pencils, and a paper the same size as the frame. She carries all this to a table and begins to trace the inset. She talks a little to a girl working next to her. By now, she has lost her sleepy look.

There seems to be some problem with A and B, the geometric solid boys, who have now been joined by a girl. It sounds like a dispute over who is going to put away what. The teacher comes by, listens a moment, says in a quiet manner "Decide that among yourselves," and moves on. The girl rolls up the rug, and the boys put the materials away. It is now nine-fifteen.

I notice a girl next to me who is washing dishes. There are two large bowls, a sponge, soap, and a pitcher, all carefully laid out. She has a bright yellow apron on. She is quite involved in what she is doing and seems to be especially enjoying the feel of the suds.

The teacher is in front of me on the floor with a little girl working with letters. They are in a wooden frame box. The consonants are blue, the vowels, red. The teacher seems to be saying a word, and the girl then makes it with letters on the rug. The little girl who had been playing with the animal comes and stands by the teacher. "Do you need help?" the teacher asks. The child is really quite young, I realize, as I see her up close. The teacher buttons her apron for her. The girl goes to get a basket from the shelf, sits at a table, carefully lays out its contents, and begins to polish a small mirror.

There is a boy using a button frame (a wooden frame with pieces of material that button together). He repeats the buttoning and unbuttoning process a number of times. It appears to be quite easy for him, and he is in no hurry. He looks around at what the others are doing while he works.

Another girl is working intently with clay. She is sitting next to a boy who is drawing a picture with watercolor pens. He puts his work away and walks by the boy with the button frame. He says something to him, and the frame is quickly put away. They make a bit of a buzzing noise and rush about a little, so I know something is up. I half expect them to start running around, but it turns out they are just excited over what they plan to do next. "You get the rug," one boy says to the other. They get out a puzzle map of the hemispheres. (These are wooden puzzle maps, carefully hand-crafted. The edges are all smooth, and the pieces brightly painted. Tiny knobs on the pieces make them easy to handle.) They discuss where the pieces go. "No, no, no! Right here. Okay."

As all this goes on, I notice that they, and in fact all the children, are speaking in ordinary voices. There are none of the muted tones and whispers heard in some Montessori classrooms. Yet, the overall sound level is somehow not loud or obtrusive in any way. If I had to choose one word to describe the atmosphere, I would say "natural," and my second choice would be "relaxed."

I turn back to the map boys. "I know we need this," I hear. Then one goes to the teacher, who cuts some paper for them the size of the puzzle map. They both almost run for colored pencils, and there is some discussion of colors. "I'll get orange, etc." They take a bowl, return to the rug, and trace two circles the size of the hemisphere map. One boy begins to make a map of the Western hemisphere by tracing pieces from the puzzle in one of the circles; the other does the Eastern hemisphere in the other. They then begin to color the drawings, using the same colors for the continents as the wooden map does.

I see a little girl with a block into which movable cylinders fit.

She has taken the cylinders (which are graduated in size) out of their holes and placed them in front of the block. She drops a tiny one and gets up to retrieve it. She seems to be watching what others around her are doing as she works. She is at one of the individual tables in the room, but other children are nearby, some also at tables and some on rugs on the floor.

Next to me, the little girl at the bells says aloud, but seemingly to herself, "These bells don't seem the right way put together to me. Let's try them again." Two other girls come up, and they talk for a few minutes as she continues with the bells. (There are two sets of bells: one arranged so that the sound each bell makes corresponds to the next note in the scale, the other arranged by the child to match the first set.

Gradually, I become aware of another sound in the room: "Beep, beep, beep," one boy is saying. He is at a table, and I can't see what he is doing. A boy goes between this table and another with a tray on which there are two porcelain pitchers. He is careful, but the other boy is causing a minor disturbance with his "beeping." The boy with the pitchers sits at a farther table and begins to pour water from pitcher to pitcher with great care, using a funnel. The teacher comes up to a girl next to the beeping boy and helps her rearrange her pencils. (She is tracing a metal inset.) She (the teacher) then speaks to the beeping boy very quietly. I cannot hear what she says. But the next moment he is crying, and she has picked him up. He is resting his head on her shoulder. There is an obvious warmth and tenderness in their relationship. The teacher carries the boy into a small room adjoining the classroom. In a few minutes she is back, still carrying him. They go to a tissue box. She hands him a tissue and puts him down. He blows his nose, wipes his eyes with his hands, goes to the small room to throw the tissue away, and returns to his table. Whatever happened, he seems back together again. I think once more how small he is. He must be barely three.

Another girl is sitting at a table, folding squares of material along sewn-in lines to make triangles, squares, and other shapes. She works with great concentration. Next to her the girl with the cylinders continues working and watching. The girl washing dishes is now beginning to clean up. She brings in a bucket for the dishwater. The assistant teacher is working with a boy with movable letters, a different box from the one used by the teacher and the girl earlier. These letters are smaller, and she appears to be asking for sounds, not whole words. The map boys are working away on the floor, talking to each other at the same time. Another girl is looking at a paperback book of reptiles.

It is now nine-thirty, and I go into another room. This time the children are five to seven years old. They seem busy, but again in a relaxed and sociable fashion. There are several children working on rugs on the floor by the door. They are making books of the continents. I notice that the continents are the same size as those traced by the younger children in the first room. These youngsters have apparently used the same map as an outline. They have written the names of the continents on the book covers, which are spread out on the rugs together with pictures to be pasted on them representing life in each continent. The children also have lined paper, and they tell me they are going to write a story about each continent for their books. Since several children seem to be working on this same project, I ask if they are all going to do it. "Yes," say the girls next to me, who are busy getting snacks out of their lunchboxes on the floor. Just then a boy comes up to the teacher and says, "I'm ready to do my continent book now." That answers my next question, which is "Who chooses when to do what?" There seems to be a good deal of eating going on at various tables. Work is out everywhere, too, but a fair amount of it appears to have been abandoned for the moment in favor of the snacks.

This room, I notice, is not as simple as the first room. It is far from cluttered, but there is more on the walls. Also, the shelves go up higher, which creates a fuller impression. Many materials are the same as those used by the younger children.

A child comes up to the teacher who has brought me to the room. She hugs her. "I can't touch you," the child tells her. "I have gooey hands." (Cupcakes seem to be a favorite snack.) Gradually, I notice, work is being returned to as the snacks are finished.

A boy comes up to where the group is working on the continent maps. He unrolls his rug, causing the pictures which one girl had laid out to paste, to blow about. "Sorry about that, Noel," the boy tells her. "Tom, I'm going to punch you," she replies. But her tone is casual. "Now, don't do that again," she cautions him, "Look out, you're stepping on Brian's." (He was, in fact, but barely. He was actually trying not to.) "Too bad," he answers. "You mess everything up," she complains, but her still-gentle tone sounds more like flirting. "Yeah, but you hadn't pasted yet," says Tom, getting back to the crux of the matter. Now the girl closest to Noel says, "You don't know how hard it is for me to sleep at night. I have a baby brother. He sleeps right next to me." The conversation turns casual.

The teacher shows the boy who was "ready" to start his continent book how to go about it. They have a hemisphere map (like the one in the first room) on the rug, but this one has two knobs missing. That's not ideal. That is, however, the only missing part I notice in any equipment that morning. I think about the amount of work involved in keeping all the materials in good condition, and the collecting of all those pictures to be pasted. Later I notice an assistant and several children cutting out pictures. So that's how the teacher manages that, I think, at least for this particular project.

I walk about. A boy is working on the stamp game. This is math material and consists of a box of small tablets with numbers on them. On his paper the boy has written "five plus two is seven." The box lid says "Steven's fact box." He is still eating, and I feel that he is not particularly happy with his work. Next to him are several tables. At one a girl is doing decimal work with a wooden chart. Another is working with a stamp game.

Nearby, one girl is sitting with a closed reference book in front of her. Thinking she really isn't engaged with anything at the moment, and that such a reference book is a bit much for even a six or seven year old, I ask her what she is doing. She opens the book promptly to a page that has a marker in it. "Oh," she says, "we're going to write a story, and then we're going to build a tunnel of mud up there in the front of the room and plunge a stick in it, and rocks fly out." Needless to say, the picture in the book is of a volcano. I'm impressed with the very confident, but nice and warm, manner in which she describes all this to me. A boy comes up to her with some paper, for writing the story. "Oh, that's plenty," she tells him.

I kneel down by a table where a girl is still eating her cupcake. "Land forms," she says to me without being asked, her legs swinging back and forth under the table. "You color them in. One is named an isthmus." There are papers with a peninsula and other land forms outlined on them on the table. There are also cards with definitions on them: "A gulf is a large part of an ocean or sea extending. . . ." She has copied one of the definitions on a piece of paper. I know that her first introduction to land forms when she was in a Montessori classroom for younger children, was through trays in which the land forms were built up of clay and she poured water into the open spaces—thus creating her own gulfs, peninsulas, or whatever.

A boy walks by another table and a girl drops her colored pencils. (There are as many as five children working very closely at tables.) "Oh, Maria, pick them up," one girl says to another working with her. Then, to the boy, she says "Would you get to your work?" "We're just starting our work and now they have to start bugging us," she tells the other girl. "You guys are being too nosy," she goes on. Again, there is a teasing, flirting quality to the children's voices, as there was in the confrontation between Tom and Noel.

My "land form" girl now talks to me again. "Andre is doing the same thing," she says, pointing to a boy several tables away. He has in fact done a number of written definitions.

A girl standing by a boy doing a decimal chart says, "I kiss your mother sometimes." "Okay," he replies. "So you appreciate mothers."

A girl comes up to me. "What are you writing?" she asks. "Oh well," she says, "I'm doing the thousand chain." She goes back to the corner of the room. I notice there are four chains out. (These are chains of small glass beads for counting. The thousand chain is in bars of ten beads. There is a chain for nines, eights, and so on. There are also matching cubes of a thousand, squares of a hundred, and so on. All these are used in the counting process to show what a thousand is, what a hundred is, and so on.) The girl begins to count the beads, marking each bar with a counter and the appropriate numeral. The particular chain she is using extends most of the length of the room. It is on the floor on a long felt mat. A little boy working on another chain says, "sixty, sixty, sixty," as he searches for the counter he needs. "I'm doing the longest chain," the girl says. "That's the easiest one!" he replies. "Yeah, easiest but the longest," she answers, undaunted.

One boy is practicing writing in script, and another girl is writing spelling words. Neither has a workbook. Otherwise, the approach to spelling seems conventional in this particular classroom.

A girl is writing a story to go with a picture she has drawn. She is talking to the boy next to her, who is doing land forms, as she works. Next to them is a girl writing numerals and defining them: "twenty-five means two tens and five units. . . ." She has no numerical material out, but I know that she has probably learned these concepts originally from teen boards (wooden boards with numerals on them and tablets that slide into place making a number). These are used in conjunction with the glass bead bars.

It is time for me to leave, and I slip out quietly.

Obviously, Montessori classrooms in which the children are so plainly self-disciplined and self-motivated and the atmosphere so filled with purposeful activity and sociability as the ones I've described don't just happen. Considerable preparation is required on the part of the teacher—who must study Montessori theory, learn to observe children and their spontaneous development, and develop considerable organizational skills. In addition to this preparation, the key to success for a Montessori teacher lies in his or her ability to understand the role of the "teacher." Montessori herself substituted the terms "director or directress" for teacher. They are not often used in English translations of Montessori literature because these terms are generally used today to refer to administrative heads of organizations and could therefore be misleading. However, Montessori's original idea cannot be stressed enough: The teacher is not to teach; he or she is to guide the child—to *plan* its education for it.

Teachers should gradually introduce very young children of two-and-a-half and three years to more and more materials, extending the range of their options from one toy or one kind of material to one toy and two kinds of materials, and so on. Extending their options gradually gives the children an opportunity to be successful in choosing activities they are ready for, and therefore enjoy. In this way, their confidence in their ability to choose for themselves grows. They also learn that they can trust their teachers to present them with challenges, but not to overwhelm them with activities which they have no idea how to carry out, and which must inevitably end in frustration or boredom. The security this knowledge gives them makes them eager for new experiences.

The future success of the relationship between teachers and children in Montessori classes will depend on the teachers' ability to choose new challenges wisely. They must use their powers of observation, their knowledge of sensitive periods, and their understanding of the Montessori material. They must direct the children, but on the basis of their own observations of the children's needs. In this sense, it is the children who must direct the adults. It is not, therefore, a case of the director and the directed. The adults and the children work together to further the children's development. Thus, both are directors and both are directed.

INDEX